Addiction
"Aunt Jacky"

Addiction
"Aunt Jacky"

Rana Ryan

Addiction Publishing
New York City
www.ConsultwithRanaRyan.com

Addiction "Aunt Jacky"
Published by:
Addiction Publishing
Email: Addictionauntjacky@gmail.com
Website: www.ConsultwithRanaRyan.com

Rana Ryan, Publisher
Yvonne Rose/Quality Press, Production Coordinator
Printed Page, Cover & Interior Layout / Design

All rights reserved. No part of this publication may be reproduced, stored in a retrieval system or transmit ted in any form or by any means, electronic, mechanical, photocopying, recording or otherwise, without the prior written permission of the publisher.

This book is a work of fiction. Names, characters, places organizations, names of places, locales and places of interest are fictional.

Addiction books are available at special discounts for bulk purchases, sales promotions, fund raising or educational purposes. Email: Addictionauntjacky@gmail.com or call: 646-462-1026.

Copyright © 2018 and 2022 by Rana Ryan
ISBN#: 978-0-615-38066-7
Library of Congress Control Number: 2018907171

Dedication

To my mother Brenda Ryan who understands me more than I think she does. The perfect woman who made it through life her way. The woman who taught me everything about life through her actions. The woman who taught me what it meant to be strong, proud and how to stand on my own. The woman who people ask to be like and the women who is misunderstood.

I love you mommy, I love you mommy.

Addiction "Aunt Jacky"

Acknowledgements

I would like to thank my husband who always inspired me to write what I wanted to write about.

I want to thank my son who always believed in me even when at times I did not believe in me.

I want to thank social work for allowing me to see people in different stages of their life and giving answers to me to help them.

Addiction "Aunt Jacky"

Table of Contents

Dedication v

Acknowledgements vii

Chapter 1 : The Beginning.. 1

Chapter 2 : Trying To Grow 20

Chapter 3 : Finding Myself 37

Chapter 4 : Shit Happens 45

Chapter 5 : Dealing 55

Chapter 6 : The Bust 63

Chapter 7 : Growing Up 72

Chapter 8 : Independence 82

Chapter 9 : Hanging Tuff 92

Chapter 10 : Old Enough to Know................................... 100

Chapter 11 : Feelings Change 114

Chapter 12 : The End of the Beginning 122

About the Author 127

Order Form.. 131

Addiction "Aunt Jacky"

*I believe evil happens to everyone.
All of us, at one time or another,
experience some type of trauma that we never forget.
This trauma affects a person's life.
Even if we block it out of our minds,
it exhibits itself in the behaviors we call our own.*

Chapter 1

The Beginning

I knew it was coming, but I never saw the date. I always wondered if it would happen to me.

Since I was a social worker for seven years and a supervisor in the same field for seven years, I always thought I could catch it before it was too late. Even before I became a social worker, I realize now that all the signs were there. It should have happened with all the things Aunt Jacky had gotten herself into. But I guess we were all in denial, hoping the problem would go away. But you can't close your eyes and wish two kids away.

It all started when Aunt Jacky gave birth to her first child Brandy. Aunt Jacky became pregnant while she was hanging out, smoking weed and smoking crack. At twenty-five, she refused to work; she lived off her mother, sold drugs, stole from her mother and stole from all other family members that were dumb enough to lay their pocketbooks down in front of her.

Aunt Jacky was the type of person that never allowed herself to grow. She had everything a ghetto kid could dream of. She had big strong brothers to protect her, she had a drug-free mother who adored her and she grew up in a large middle class home in Brooklyn.

Aunt Jacky stands 5 feet 9 inches and was always chubby. Her light skin glistened across her round full face. She wasn't bad to look at, she was actually pretty. She had long black hair that she would wear in two corn braids. She had light colored eyes like me and my mother.

However she would always, in her mind, remain ghetto; loving the streets, the night life and getting into everything from running numbers to sneaking her mother's car to making drug runs in the middle of the night. Even though Aunt Jacky's family had a large house in Brooklyn, they lived on the south side of Brooklyn. This meant working-class blacks had to live amongst the drug addicts, liquor stores on every corner, as well as the high levels of crime. Aunt Jacky soaked up all the negative parts of the south side, not the lovely parts, such as: the beautiful parks, the good schools, the kids who rode bikes for fun, the rich ethnic culture and the car drives to McBee's for burgers and shakes. Aunt Jacky ran with the gangs, the drug users, drug sellers, robbers and prostitutes. Aunt Jacky is now in her early 50's but when she was a teenager she ran through people like she owned them. As long as I could remember, she was a bad seed.

Don't get me wrong; what attracted me to Aunt Jacky was the fact that she was exciting to be around. Everyone, after a while, wanted to know Jack a Lack - that was one of her nicknames. She was the person you would go see if you wanted anything and everything to happen. She was always down for anything. She would help rob banks, steal credit cards and shop with it like it was hers. She could manipulate you and you would not even know it. She got me personally, thousands of times, and she is even getting me right now at this moment. Sometimes I think she is laughing to herself and saying: "I got that Dumb Bitch!"

Aunt Jacky has fooled me over and over, since I was a child. When I was seven years old, I attended St. Bella Catholic School and I was in the second grade. Grandma, Aunt Jacky's mom gave me three hundred dollars to pay my tuition. I asked Aunt Jacky to put the money in my knapsack which was on my back at the time. I ran the two blocks to my school to pay my tuition but when I got to school the money was not there. I was sent home from school because of insufficient funds. My grandmother thought I lost the money and I got a terrible beating for that. Aunt Jacky had to be about 16 years old at the time. I was devastated because she was my favorite aunt and the person I loved and trusted the most. I would have never imagined her doing that to me. At first, I actually thought I lost the money; but I knew she took it because I ran straight to school after she put the money in the knapsack and when I got to school to give the money in, it was gone. I never took that knapsack off my back until I reached the school. Aunt Jacky never thought about me, she never thought about how hard it was for grandma, her mother, to raise that tuition money. She was selfish then and she is even more selfish now. But I didn't learn from that incident.

It was easy to look up to Aunt Jacky. She was exciting, convincing and, at times, I needed to be around someone. I continued to look up to Aunt Jacky even after that incident. I trusted her because I had no one else in my life at that time that I could trust. I had no one to go to with my problems. My mother, Aunt Jacky's sister had abandoned me and my sister when we were small babies. My mother was married to my father and soon after he divorced her, he split and so did she.

Aunt Jacky actually never helped me with anything, but she was all I had. Once, I made the mistake of asking her for help with my homework; and when I got to school, it was all wrong. I got in trouble because the teacher actually thought I completed the homework on my own and I looked stupid in front of that teacher. I still did not learn.

How could I walk away from her when she was the only person who was there for me? At least I believed that she was there for me. When my mother left, Aunt Jacky and grandma cared for my sister and me. Aunt Jacky cared for us while grandma worked to put food on the table. I had no choice.

Aunt Jacky always took me under her wing; people thought I was her daughter because we looked so much alike. She took me everywhere and I was exposed to things I had never imagined existed. For some reason being with Aunt Jacky seemed like fun; that was the only fun I knew because I had no other form of company.

My mom was out there and my dad abandoned us. I did not know any better and if she would have said the sky was black all the time I would have believed her. I thought she would have protected me because she was around; I thought she really cared for me.

Addiction "Aunt Jacky"

But the truth is that half the shit Aunt Jacky put me through, I would not wish on my worst enemy.

The first time I became really affected by Aunt Jacky's behavior was when Aunt Jacky took me out for an adventure when I was about twelve years old. She and I went out to meet a friend of hers, she explained that this friend of hers was going to give her some money and she would give me some if I tagged along with her.

I did go and we met with two guys. One was much older, possibly 35 or 40 years old, and the other one was about 22 years old. We met these two guys in an old dirty hotel downtown in the City. The hotel had dirty walls and it was hot and smoky. It had an odor that seemed familiar but nothing I remember smelling before. Aunt Jacky yelled out, "Phew wee", it smells like old tricks were using this room to fuck and smoke crack. It was dark and creepy. All I can remember was Aunt Jacky introducing me to the young one and leaving me alone with him. I felt like I was in a dream.

The room was big, it was L shaped and it had two beds. I remember seeing white sheets and that was it. I remember the guy taking me where Aunt Jacky couldn't see me anymore but it did not matter because she was not looking for me. She was glad she brought me because her friend was happy and that way she got more money.

I was alone on the other side of the room with this man and it seemed darker. I began hearing him talk very sweet to me. His face felt sweaty when he tried to kiss me and I pulled away. He began to stroke me in places I only touched when I washed. I never had real sex before, so I was very nervous. Even though I was nervous he made me feel good when he whispered in my ear. He said things to me no man ever said to me. He told me I was beautiful and that my body felt like a flower blossoming in the sun. I hated my body, I was fat, light skinned and I was round like a ball. But, I felt good and wanted more, even though I was scared; I thought I was going to pee on myself. I could not say anything, I was afraid.

The Beginning

I wanted to call Aunt Jacky, but I thought Aunt Jacky would get mad or the man would get angry if I tried calling Aunt Jacky to rescue me. I thought we were just picking up some cash. I decided to call Aunt Jacky and when I called her she responded by saying, "shut the fuck up". After I heard that I froze because the guy knew then he had me and he did.

He began kissing me, tearing at my clothes and that is when I started to fight him off. He got angry and forced himself on me. He stopped being gentle and became a mad man. He ripped off my blouse and started sucking my nipples. I never had anyone suck my nipples before. It was so erotic; my panties were so wet I thought I peed on myself but I didn't. I was aroused by the sucking of my nipples.

He then began to put his hand on my pants and started rubbing my vagina area. I freaked out because I knew if he touched me down there it was over. I knew going down in my pants would make me weak. I began to fight harder and that increased his obsession, he actually enjoyed when I fought him off. He laughed while popping the zipper off my pants and when he pulled my pants down he took a deep breath and released hot air onto my neck like a vampire.

He then touched my clit through my panties and it felt like I had no panties on. It felt so powerful; I thought I was going to explode in his arms. He knew exactly what to do to ease my tensions. He saw the frown coming off my face once he slid his hand up and down my young wet clit. I knew he had me then so I let myself go.

From then on I could not be me any longer; I had to block everything out of my mind. Once I regained my composure I noticed that his pants were off and all my clothes were off. I was cold and I started to shiver as he got closer. I knew something big was going to happen and it was not just going to be touching like before. This will actually be sex and I was scared to death.

He saw that I was a virgin and tried to be gentle. He realized I was too tight and he did not force it in. He became tired of me screaming,

"Stop!" and he must have felt sorry for me because he stopped. I knew from that night on I would never enjoy sex with a man in my life. So, he took his dick out of me laid it on my stomach and pushed and pushed and pushed until he squirted out some sticky, hot, milky stuff. I was so glad to see that stuff because he stopped after that and fell fast asleep.

Aunt Jacky ran into the room looking at me like everything was cool, meaning the guy she was with fell asleep and she had all his money. My guy also fell asleep so I grabbed my ripped clothes and we ran out the hotel, jumped into grandma's car and drove home.

Aunt Jacky never had any intentions on just getting money from these men. Her intention was for us to have sex with these men and rob them once they were asleep. I figured it out once we got in the car and she said, "You did good kid!" That bothered me so much because once we did get into the car Aunt Jacky said, "Give me the brown paper bag" and when I opened it, it was full of money. Aunt Jacky, of course, gave me about twenty-five dollars out of the five hundred dollars that she stole from both men.

I was so angry and it was not about the money. She never warned me, she set me up. She never asked me if I was sexually active. She did not care about me with this strange man. She never cared that a grown ass man had his way with me. I hated the fact that I was pushed into it; I did not have a choice because she brought me there to have sex with this man. I felt ashamed and angry at myself. I felt betrayed by Aunt Jacky and the man because I was a kid, not a woman and they took advantage of me.

This is the woman who I called my favorite aunt for many years. I was drawn to this woman and it was not just that I was alone all the time, felt unattractive and what they call a cry baby, but I felt I needed her. I believed in her. She was the one who could make things happen. Why when we are kids we see one thing about a person and not the other. I believe I would have saved myself so much grief if I had just walked away from Aunt Jacky.

The Beginning

In second grade, Aunt Jacky introduced me to weed. She said it was cool; it was happening, it was good for you. She smoked weed all the time and she wanted a partner. I became her sidekick. She wanted someone under her belt and I was the student. I got an A+ on my efforts with Aunt Jacky.

What do you do when you find out the person who molested you for years threatened to tell your family? But the scary part is you do not realize that some one in your family already knows. I found out years later that Aunt Jacky knew that her boyfriend was trying to molest me for over two years, starting when I was nine years old. Even until this day I would run from him when I see him in the streets. I am still afraid of him and this happened over thirty-five years ago. I remember once when I was in the shopping mall with my friends, I was about 16 years old and I saw him. I ran to the car and left my friends standing there in the middle of the mall. Until this day, I am ashamed of what had happened. I could not tell my sister, nor could I tell my mother. I could not tell Aunt Jacky so the secret stayed with me my entire life.

When my family would invite Aunt Jacky's boyfriend over I would just leave the house. No one would even bother to notice that something was wrong with me and if they did notice I would have not felt secure enough to explain. He would threaten me by saying he would tell my family that I wanted to have sex with him and I was acting out sexually in front of him. But he was the one who started the whole fucking thing. He used to stare at me but I never paid it any mind. He used to touch me funny so I stayed away from him. I had to be no more than eight years old when I first realized the funny touching was bad. He was an asshole. He would first visit with Aunt Jacky and once he had sex with her, he would go home and call me while she slept.

He lived close to our home. I could not escape him. When the phone calls first started I did not know it was him. He would say things like, "are you touching your pussy"? I would not respond and then he would hang up. That was my first sexual experience. I never felt so stimulated. My body and my brains were on fire. I was scared but I would always go back to the phone to answer it. The phone calls were getting scarier but more and more exciting. He would call and say nasty things to me and it turned me on. I did what he asked over the phone even though I knew it was wrong, but it appeared harmless at first. He would call and say nice things at first and then it turned in to things like, "I like your pretty ass and it's beautiful." By the time I turned nine years old I fell into a trap that almost killed me emotionally. I became hooked to the phone calls and I could not wait to answer the phone. It seemed like when I picked up the phone it was always him. It became unbearable to live with the shame and the guilt. I did things over the phone that a nine year old would have never done. But it was something I became addicted to. It was my first addiction.

When this phone person revealed himself, I became more ashamed and withdrawn. He had changed his voice and I did not know it was Aunt Jacky's boyfriend. Once I found out it was him, he would tell me that the phone calls would be reported to Aunt Jacky and my family and I would be in big trouble if I did not continue.

I knew it was wrong to enjoy the phone calls, but after a while I felt addicted to them and I couldn't hang up. It was Aunt Jacky's boyfriend getting me ready to be his next victim. He knew if he got me hooked on the phone calls first, he would have something on me to threaten me with and it worked. I felt I had to submit to him because he had dirt on me that I considered death. My family would have killed me if they found out that I was listening to dirty talk over the phone. I never thought at that time that it was not my fault. He dragged the phone sex into something worse and I hated him even more for that.

Finally, Aunt Jacky decide to dump the sorry ass molester whom she dated for years; but it didn't mean he was not still a part of the family. The family thought of his family as "good people". I had to see the stinking bastard for years to come. I never imagined that one phone call would get me in so much trouble. The phone calls started to become boring to him and eventually he tried to have sex with me.

The Beginning

I thought I would be free because we lost our home in Brooklyn and we had to move to Staten Island. I thought that my secret was safe and I could move on, but he had something bigger in store for me. He told grandma that he would come over to help us pack and move to our new home in Staten Island. He came over and helped us pack. He kept staring at me, telling me to come in the other room with him; he was very brave. I refused but that meant nothing to him. He loved the fact that I was getting older, that I was 10 years old going on 11 years old.

Grandma decided to let him help us move to Staten Island. He assisted in all the packing and we got everything packed quickly. The next thing I remembered is being on the moving truck heading to Staten Island. Everyone was tired when we got to Staten Island, so we all went straight to bed after unloading the moving truck. Grandma asked him to stay overnight so he could take the moving truck back to Brooklyn in the morning.

Everybody was asleep, but not him, because he was trying to sneak into the bedroom where I was sleeping. I closed my door and I tried to lock it but it had no lock. When he saw that I closed the door, he went back into the living room. I then felt safe enough to fall asleep but after falling into a deep sleep I was awakened by him caressing me. I woke up in a cold sweat. He whispered to me to touch his dick but it was so big and ugly I wanted to throw up. I eventually touched it and then he asked me to kiss it. I said, "No"!

He frowned and pushed my head down on it and I was going to scream but my mouth was full of dick. It tasted horrible and I tried to get up and he held my head down. I then jumped up out of the bed and ran into the bathroom and locked the door. I was so scared. I cried myself to sleep on the bathroom floor. I felt hurt like I never felt before. I felt alone and that no one cared. I could not tell my story and I needed to. I kept it all to myself. He went back into the living room and went to sleep.

Morning came and he acted as if nothing was wrong. I could not look at him, but I knew I felt stronger to fight him if I had to. That morning, my grandmother asked him to take the moving truck back to the company. He took the truck back to Brooklyn and grandma never had a reason to call him over again. He started to give up on trying to have sex with me. The phone calls continued but I could tell he was bored and he wanted sex. I kept hanging up on him and that was the one thing I had control over and he knew it. I believe he realized that if he had sex with me and I was unwilling, I could get hurt and he would go to jail. So, after traveling to my house a couple of more times begging me to have sex with him, he finally gave up. All I could say was "Thank GOD". He became more and more tired of coming to Staten Island on the ferry. He was running out of excuses of why he was coming to my home. He and Aunt Jacky, by then, were through. My family did start to get suspicious and thought he wanted money or something. Of course, Aunt Jacky never noticed a thing; she was in Aunt Jacky's land.

By the time we moved to Staten Island, Aunt Jacky became crazier. She dropped out of school, she had no plans to get a job and she started stealing the family's car more often. She never worked and she always leeched. Anybody and everybody who had money was Aunt Jacky's friend. By the time I became an adolescent I was earning my Ph.D. in the streets after Aunt Jacky raised me. Aunt Jacky was the one who taught me how to be cool, so I thought the things I did were cool. I thought cutting classes and smoking pot was the thing to do. Staten Island changed me, I was not in Catholic School any longer and I was forced to attend public school.

Before the crack epidemic came about Aunt Jacky was considered the coolest thing that hit the streets since rap music. She knew all the cool places to hang out, she knew where to get drugs and if you'd say her name on the right block, you would get mad respect. As time went on, I saw less of Aunt Jacky. Aunt Jacky's mind, body and spirit were disappearing. She started going to jail for her crimes. She did small time, nothing hard; but her name was becoming familiar with the local police in Staten Island. So, she was never comfortable living in one place. She kept moving around because she knew that she could not commit crimes where she lived unless she was desperate. She did not feel the desperation at this time. She was still young and was able to move around as she pleased.

She met a big time local drug dealer who owned apartment buildings and his family owned the apartment building we lived in, in Staten Island. It was not easy for us coming from owning two homes in Brooklyn to renting out a slum apartment in Staten Island. I had to attend public school for the first time, which was very difficult for me. I was used to attending private schools. Even though I considered the apartment to be a slum, it was a great apartment. But coming from a home, it was hard for me and my family to adjust.

Things got really bad when grandma no longer could keep the two homes. Between bailing her children out of jail and putting the homes up for col lateral so many times it finally caught up with the family finances. We were not used to being broke. We were used to having a home we could rent and a home we could live in. The homes grandma owned in Brooklyn were Brownstones. They were huge; these were Brownstones with three apartments in one building. These were properties my grandmother thought she was going to be able to leave to her grandchildren. My grandmother was devastated, but ironically she never showed how hurt she was. You can only feel how hurt she was and I felt it because we were connected.

The family's breadwinner was grandma; but unfortunately she could not carry the household without the drug money. My mother was either in jail or abandoning the family again. Aunt Jacky was stealing everything in sight and grandma's sons who were drug dealers were either in jail or on the run.

Aunt Jacky decided to hook up with the drug dealer she met. His family owned the building we were living in which was convenient for all of us. This worked in our favor because we did get the largest apartment in the building, it had four bedrooms. Aunt Jacky fell in love with this man; he gave her money, drugs and more fame on the block. She could not be happier. This was the type of man that Aunt Jacky could fall in love with.

Addiction "Aunt Jacky"

His name was Dexter and he was small in stature and Aunt Jacky loved that about him. She always joked that she could beat him up if she had to. But Aunt Jacky really loved him and he showed his love for her, of course, by buying her and the family gifts. They would go on trips together, dancing, skating, normal things Aunt Jacky was not used to doing. Even though Aunt Jacky grew up in a home where all of those things were promoted, she just did not take a liking to them. I remember grandma buying Aunt Jacky ice skates and enrolling her into piano and tap dancing classes, but Aunt Jacky just wanted to be in the streets.

There was something different with this new guy Dexter that Aunt Jacky noticed. He may have been a drug dealer and ran with gangsters, but he wanted his wife at home with him. He failed to realize that Aunt Jacky was the type of young woman who wanted to be a gangster; she wanted to carry guns and pistol whip people for money. She loved the con game and practically made a living from it. Dexter did not like the drug game; he wanted to continue to buy property and legitimize his business. He even stopped using drugs to get his life together. However, Aunt Jacky continued to do drugs and she was hanging out even more.

Dexter brought Aunt Jacky her own car and she was on the go staying out two and three days at a time. Aunt Jacky was used to driving, since she had her first car at 16 years old. She wasn't even out of high school and she was balling with a brand new Volkswagen Buggy, white on white with leather interior. Within a year the car was totaled. Aunt Jacky blamed it on her girlfriend; and being spoiled, of course, grandma did not ask questions. I guess grandma was just glad Aunt Jacky was alive and she did not kill anyone. At least, that is what she believed at the time. Later on, we found out that Aunt Jacky almost did kill someone after leaving the club scene drunk and drag racing.

Aunt Jacky began to act different. Dexter was stressing her to stay home more often. She started to slow down and everyone kept wondering what had happened that made her come home and act as if she wanted to be there. She would sleep all day and then she would cook and eat practically all night. Dexter was happy, he thought he changed her and he was feeling good and even happy for once in their relationship. Aunt Jacky surprised everyone. We were all happy and thought she was trying to save her relationship and her life. Grandma was praying that she would stay that way. I think she really was trying, but it was too hard for her.

I guess Aunt Jacky felt she could not hide it any longer. So, she made the announcement one night while we were all sitting around smoking weed in the house. She said, "I am two months pregnant" while she was smoking a joint and getting ready to light a cigarette. I did not know anyone who was pregnant before. I really did not understand what that meant at that time, so I was confused especially after smoking a joint. Dexter just stood there and looked more confused than I was. Aunt Jacky yelled at me and Dexter for not acknowledging her statement.

Grandma was at work; my sister was asleep so I had no one to ask what Aunt Jacky was talking about. Aunt Jacky told me to get out of the room; she said it was my bed time. I laughed to myself thinking *I know she is crazy.* I never had a bedtime when I hung out with Aunt Jacky and now she is giving me one. All I heard next was, "get the hell out of here" and I ran to my room. I kept my door open to hear them yelling at each other about Aunt Jacky's announcement.

From what I could gather, Dexter was mad that Aunt Jacky knew she was pregnant and continued to get high. Dexter yelled at Aunt Jacky. He said that she was killing his child. Aunt Jacky yelled back that she would stop getting high. I was scared because I never saw them argue like that before. I went to the bathroom and I saw Dexter throwing Aunt Jacky's cigarettes, the weed and anything else he could find that would harm the baby in the trash.

I was sad that Aunt Jacky was having a baby; I thought she would dump me for her new life. Even though Aunt Jacky treated me bad most of the time, she was the closest thing I had to a mother. Then it became quiet. Aunt Jacky and Dexter must have gone to bed. I went back into the living room and watched the late show. I found half a joint in the garbage and smoked it by myself.

The next morning everyone seemed or acted as if they were happy. Aunt Jacky looked relieved that she shared her secret and her old face reappeared. I had to take a double look because I could tell it took courage for her to admit to being pregnant and I knew she did not mean a word of her promise to stop getting high. Dexter was in his glory; he was calling his mother who lived in Panama, his sisters and just enjoying the moment. On the other hand, Aunt Jacky looked as if she could not wait to hit the streets and party. Everyone in my family was happy for Aunt Jacky. We all felt that she would slow down and take care of herself since she was pregnant.

Four months have passed and Dexter started traveling more and more to and from Panama. Aunt Jacky was having a serious problem with Dexter not being there to cater to her needs. She was using that as an excuse to start getting high while she was pregnant. She started smoking cigarettes heavier than before and wasn't satisfied that Dexter gave her, her own apartment in the building as a gift for her and the baby. She complained the entire time she was moving into the apartment about Dexter traveling and leaving her alone during her pregnancy. Dexter had the apartment fully furnished and the baby's room finished with the help of his sister because Aunt Jacky was not into all that. Aunt Jacky barely stayed at the apartment. She mostly stayed with us; especially when Dexter was out of town. It was easier for her to lie to Dexter when he called their apartment and she was not there. She would say she stayed over at her family's house.

Before Aunt Jacky hit her seventh month she was staying out all night, even when Dexter was in town. She started to not care again and it was ugly. Dexter would come over in the middle of the night looking for her and we all knew what was going on, but of course no one said anything. Grandma would say stupid shit like, "maybe she fell asleep at one of her girlfriend's houses".

Aunt Jacky did not realize that as she continued to get high off the drugs and party, her boyfriend decided it was quits. She assumed that he wanted a drug-addicted dictator whose idea of working was going out to steal another person's pocketbook and use it as if it was her own. Aunt Jacky did not realize the thing with drug dealers is that, you can get high with your man; but after a while they do expect you to stop. Even if they are getting high with you, they look at you differently because they want you to be different from the women they are selling drugs to and the people they are getting high with. I learned that men really want smart women who don't do drugs and have careers. Usually when couples get high together the woman usually ends up a junkie and the man ends up clean. The man gets clean and marries a woman who never even heard of pot or crack cocaine. So, Aunt Jacky did not see it coming, she was living well, spending his money, driving his car and of course she was not working.

Dexter waited until after Aunt Jacky gave birth before he dumped her. Dexter expected her to clean up her act and I guess he wanted to see how she would behave knowing this was her first child and his first child. Aunt Jacky gave birth to a beautiful daughter and she named her Brandy. Aunt Jacky named her first born after alcohol because she said she loved drinking warm G&B Brandy on cold winter days. Brandy was beautiful; but Aunt Jacky was so far gone she never appreciated how beautiful her daughter was. I do not think she spent a day with her daughter when she was born because she was born with a positive toxicology test, meaning Brandy had drugs in her system so she could not go home with Aunt Jacky.

Brandy had to be escorted out of the hospital by Aunt Jacky's mother, grandma. Aunt Jacky's personal life was falling apart around her. Once Dexter told her it was over, he kicked her out of the apartment and he moved back to Panama. He saw Brandy once before he left but he got fed up with the fact that his daughter was born with drugs in her system.

Addiction "Aunt Jacky"

Aunt Jacky seemed not to care, she did not have to take responsibility for her child and she was free from her relationship. That was Aunt Jacky's opportunity to do what she wanted and that is what she did. Rather than seeing this as an opportunity to get help, Aunt Jacky saw this as an opportunity to leave everything and everyone behind.

Aunt Jacky was not in the relationship for love but for financial support. Dexter realized that Aunt Jacky did not care about him or the baby. Once he cut her off financially she thought she would hurt him by hurting the baby, by leaving the baby in grandma's care. Aunt Jacky wanted to get him back for taking everything and leaving her. She was mean in that way, she could not rest until she got him back. Leaving her child wasn't enough.

Aunt Jacky called Dexter and apologized. She asked him to come to dinner to talk about the baby. She even volunteered to cook for Dexter after the breakup and he agreed to a nice dinner to discuss their relationship. Aunt Jacky's intentions were to hurt Dexter; she was not interested in their relationship. Aunt Jacky on the night she invited Dexter for dinner pissed in his collard greens and fed it to him. She laughed through the entire dinner and, even though I knew, I dared say nothing or she would have killed me.

Aunt Jacky saw she could not get any reaction from Dexter, so she tried again to hurt him by fucking his brother and she succeeded. Dexter was devastated when he found out about Aunt Jacky and his brother. Dexter's family was from Panama and his brother only visited New York twice a year. Dexter's brother was the drug supplier; he was the one with the most money. Dexter's brother loved Aunt Jacky but, for some reason not enough to marry her, only to have a good time. He always went back to see Aunt Jacky and that made Dexter furious.

Once when Dexter came to visit Brandy, he and his brother were staying at their family's home and Aunt Jacky literally fucked Dexter's brother while Dexter was in the next room. She would stay overnight at their family's home in New Jersey with her baby's father's brother. She would come home and laugh to herself saying I got my "baby daddy" mad.

The Beginning

Aunt Jacky's plan did not work. All it did was make her look even worse to Dexter and it made Dexter move on quicker. She could not get into Dexter's family, so she gave up. All this time she had been trying to win back her baby's father's love and trying to get back into the family; but Dexter completely ignored the fact that she had his daughter. Aunt Jacky needed money and his family was the target, but she failed.

Brandy was getting older and she became a burden to everyone in the house. I was damn near a teenager and I was burdened with Aunt Jacky's problems. At first, of course it was fun; I had fun helping grandma with the baby Brandy. When Aunt Jacky started leaving the house without coming back for days at a time and I would have to miss school or miss what was important to me; it was no longer fun to watch Brandy. No one ever apologized to me. It was "you have to do it or else". I never knew what the "or else" meant in my house because I never went as far as to not do what I was supposed to.

By this time, money was getting tight for everyone; the crack epidemic took everyone's money. There was less food in our house, the apartment we had appeared smaller because everyone was in and out of our home. I never had privacy or peace; Aunt Jacky and her friends ruled the house. When she came home it was a party all night, drugs, music and the next morning all she did was sleep. Grandma was the only one working a legitimate job and she worked nights, so it was hard for her to know who was coming in and out of the house at night.

I remember so clearly one morning getting ready for school when I was in the 7th grade. Aunt Jacky and her friends were smoking crack at the kitchen table at 7:00 a.m. in the morning. She gave me money and rushed me off to school. Her daughter Brandy was in the house while she was getting high with her friends. I do not know if she fed Brandy that day while I was in school.

At that time, since I was so young I enjoyed having an aunt with faults because if my school called because I was acting out, Aunt Jacky would handle it. If I wanted to get weed Aunt Jacky would get it. If I wanted to hang out all night Aunt Jacky would let me. She was the one who made the decisions for me when I was growing up. She was my caretaker. But when I was sad she was not there, when I was lonely she was not there, when I was feeling bad about myself no one was there. Aunt Jacky was there for me for the bad reasons; she was like my personal devil who I loved to hate.

When Brandy's father's mother died, money got really tight. Dexter's mother was giving Aunt Jacky some money on the side and money to grandma to help support Brandy. Also, since they owned the building our rent was cheap. After Dexter's mother died things got worse; we had to move because Dexter and his brother sold the building and they moved back to Panama permanently. Even though we had to move, grandma made sure, as always, that we had a lovely home to rent. She found a place that was the best thing since living back in Brooklyn. I was used to growing up in a house and I was glad to finally have a backyard again.

The area we moved to at that time was the better part of Staten Island. It is called Eastchester; I loved it because it had trees, charming homes, lawns and a backyard...something I was used to. I could not wait to move into that house. We had a front patio, we had friendly neighbors and we were surrounded by Puerto Ricans, which was new to me. This was the first time I saw Puerto Ricans. I never lived around them in Brooklyn or I was too young to notice or they were not around where I grew up. I loved living in Eastchester, but there were things I learned how to do there that would never leave me.

Brandy was nearly two years old before Aunt Jacky was pregnant again and by this time, Aunt Jacky was in and out of Wikers Island Correctional Facility. She stated she had a one night stand with Brandy's father and she became pregnant. That story was so bullshit. I was so mad. Aunt Jacky knew she did not take care of Brandy for the first year and a half of Brandy's life. Now, Aunt Jacky had the nerve to get pregnant again. What was I supposed to do? I was taking care of Brandy full-time already and how could I manage two kids and school.

That's when I realized, if I did not go to school I would be trapped in that house watching Brandy and her soon to be sibling forever. I never imagined that would happen to me.

Chapter 2

Trying To Grow

Aunt Jacky was in prison most of her pregnancy and when she was released she was either living with friends or staying on the streets. It appeared that she would rather go to everyone else's house except her own. By this time she was not trying to contact the family. She was still hustling and using drugs. The party did not stop just because she was pregnant. Phone calls came in here and there from her when she needed money or to see if the police came by looking for her.

I was left alone when she left; I became tired and depressed. I had to watch her daughter after school, at night and all day on Saturdays and Sundays. It was exhausting, taking care of a baby and going to school. I was up all night when Brandy refused to sleep and once she did fall asleep, I would just relax and smoke weed until I fell asleep.

I became addicted to weed and cigarettes. I was smoking everyday. I believe this is the time when I started to use drugs, just to escape. Prior to this I was using because it was there and it was supposed to be cool. This is also when I began to try new drugs because it appeared that the weed was not doing enough to ease the pain of abandonment. I was getting bored with the weed and I think it was just an excuse to smoke crack. It was all around me so I started smoking crack with my weed and the only bad part was that I could not get crack easily. It was on the downlow that I smoked crack. I could get weed easily since weed-heads were respected and crack was whack. I was embarrassed to cop crack on my own. No one knew this but me and the dealer. I would sneak and smoke crack mixed with my weed and this would only make me feel good for a moment. I would feel guilty and ashamed so I would only do it occasionally.

I started to take every dime I had to buy crack when I had the urge for it. That urge would come at least twice a month when I got real depressed. I felt it pushing its way into my life and becoming a full time addiction. It made me feel good for awhile and that's what I thought I needed to cope with my problems.

I was in the 8th grade by now and I was entering the last term. Since we moved to Staten Island I had to attend a new school and I had very few friends. I had to choose a high school and I wondered which high school would accept me. I chose Thomas Harding High School because it just turned co-ed. It was an all boy school up until the time I entered as a freshman. The ratio was one girl to ten boys. It was hard for me; but I wanted to complete the 8th grade because that meant moving on and I needed something positive to happen in my life.

As I was getting closer to eighth grade graduation, I was looking harder at myself. I hated the picture and I did not want to go into high school with a crack problem. I wasn't new to the game; I knew what crack did to you. I realized I had to put it on hold; it could not interfere with my goals which were getting into high school. I began to focus on weed and studying. I took care of Brandy, studied for my classes and I turned in my homework on time. I was determined to get out of junior high school with a diploma, not just an addiction.

I was improving in school but I thought I could not do it. This was the first time I saw myself accomplish something good. I was proud of myself. I had so much fun preparing for Thomas Harding High School. I was ready to experiment with boys my own age. I wanted my own friends to look up to me and I felt I needed to reinvent myself. I worked hard to fight that urge to smoke crack and the only way I was able to succeed at that was to smoke lots and lots of weed and cigarettes.

I was looking for everyone to notice the change in me. My teacher loved the new me. She noticed my work being handed in on time, me coming to class regularly and she was very proud of me. I felt wonderful. This was not supposed to be me, I was supposed to lose. I was supposed to drop out.

Aunt Jacky was still hanging out and not coming home, I was forced to plan my eighth grade graduation alone. I wanted everyone there, but grandma had to work a double shift the day of my graduation, cleaning white folks' homes as a second job. My mother was nowhere to be found and my father refused my phone calls. I decided to attend my graduation alone. It was the saddest and the greatest feeling I ever felt and I knew I wanted that good feeling again. I loved thinking about graduation. I loved seeing what I had accomplished and getting rewarded for it. But on the flip side, I had no one there, no one to say, "Hey, you did it". There was no one to say congratulations.

The day of graduation I was depressed. I saw some kids I knew and they were taking pictures with their families and I was there alone. Other kids were making arrangements to go to dinner with their families and I went home alone. This day meant a lot to me; this was the first time I succeeded at something and it was overwhelming. The graduation ceremony was sentimental and I was overjoyed. I was never taught how to accomplish anything in my life up until graduation. I never knew what it was like to make it. I did not feel like me at graduation, I felt like a winner. This was the day that made me realize, I can be a success and I do not have to rob anyone or steal anything to make a living. During the graduation ceremony my principal played the song "Man in the Mirror" by Michael Jackson and I cried. It forced me to look at myself.

After graduation, there was no more school for me. It was summer and I was mixed up in a variety of activities. I was babysitting all day and as soon as I got Brandy asleep I started looking for some weed to smoke. Money for crack was limited so I began to start selling some of the things that my mother stole for me. Such as designer pocketbooks, jewelry and anything that was sellable. I was becoming more and more ashamed. At night, I would try to forget about the urge to sneak and smoke crack. This is why I smoked crack in my weed; it made me feel a little better about smoking it. I did not consider myself a crack-head because, at that time, all the real crack heads smoked crack in a pipe. I would smoke crack and it would go so fast, I did not understand it; it was amazing how I fell in love with the smell of it and the taste of it. It gave me a feeling like I never experienced before.. .a feeling of love and assurance. At that time; it was the greatest feeling to me. Because I was mixing the crack with my weed, I got a better effect and I did not get addicted as quickly.

The crack and the weed comforted me. It made me feel warm inside; it felt like someone loved me. Crack is a powerful seduction. I fell in love with something that kills; and while I was smoking it, I thought about dying. Maybe I wanted to kill myself.

It was getting harder for me to afford weed, crack and cigarettes so I became more frustrated with my situation and started to think crazy. I thought I could meet men and they would give me money.

One night I was thirsty for crack and I went out for a walk late at night. I was approached by a man in a nice Volvo. He asked me my name and I gave him a bogus name, which was Michelle. He was a big man, with dark skin and a big hat. I was so nervous because he said, "get in; I will take you to dinner". I figured he was nice because he offered dinner and had a nice car. He spoke pleasantly with a soft voice. He was not intimidating at all; I thought I had this man wrapped around my finger. I was fourteen and thought I had game.

We pulled up in front of McBees and sat in the parking lot to talk. He was feeling me out by asking me, who did I live with, and how old I was. I knew he was asking me those questions to see if I had any family that could protect me on the streets. Once I said I lived with my grandmother and I was fifteen years old, his eyes lit up. I lied, I told him that I was an only child and that my grandmother left me alone to go to work without giving me dinner. He started to sweat as he gave me money to buy some McBees.

One thing about my appearance was that I always looked older. I was 5 feet eleven; I was 165 pounds with light green eyes that were visible in the dark. Folks always thought I wore contact lenses. I was big breasted and had a big ass. My body filled out and I was no longer fat. Being light-skinned with long hair also was a turn on for him.

Since the conversation was going so well, I got the nerve to ask him for money and he looked at me with a smirk on his face. It was like he was waiting for that question and he replied, "you suck my dick and I'll give you what you want". That remark snapped me right out of thinking I had him in the palm of my hand. I was never propositioned before for money and I did not know how to respond. So, I said "no", feeling insulted. He said, "You're not leaving until you suck my dick" and "now you blew the money Bitch". I could not believe I had gotten myself in this situation, I was so scared.

I thought I knew the streets because I hung around Aunt Jacky all my life. I told him I was not sucking his dick and he said, "Yes you are". I told him that he can have his fucking hamburger back; he shoved the hamburger in my face and stuffed a fifty dollar bill between my tits. I knew then he was not letting me go.

I was so mad I could have cut his dick off but I was too scared to act on it. He saw that I got scared and he grabbed my neck and zipped open his pants and all I saw was a big black stick. I thought I was going to choke if he shoved his dick down my throat. He did exactly what I thought he would do, he pushed my mouth on his big dick and he began to scream out my phony name. He started to push my head down quicker and quicker. He began to breathe heavy and that is when he got rough. He brought my head up and smacked me in the mouth for letting my teeth touch his dick. He said, "You're sucking it wrong bitch". He kept saying, "Stop using your teeth" and every time I used my teeth he would punch me in the back of my head. He then placed both of his hands on the back of my head and made me suck his dick without coming up for air. I nearly choked to death. It took a long time for him to come and when he did he came in my mouth. White stuff was flowing down the sides of my mouth and I was crying. He then threw me out of the car and called me a nasty slut.

I had to walk at least thirty-five blocks home. I cried the entire long cold walk home. But before I got home I stopped and bought $30 worth of crack cocaine $10 worth of weed and I kept $10 dollars. I do not know if it was during, before or after that night but I vowed to myself I would never use crack again. I vowed that no man would ever do that to me again. I was so angry with myself; I hated myself for a long time after that night. I knew that was the last time I would smoke crack and allow crack to do that to me. I really understood after that night what it felt like to fail, to be an underachiever, to feel like nothing matters anymore. That night I washed my mouth out with rubbing alcohol, peroxide and tooth paste. I thought long and hard about what had happened and I knew that life was not for me and I did not want to be on the street as a street walker.

The fall was near and I knew I had to get my act together if I wanted to attend high school in the right mind. It was a month before school started back and I was about to start High School. I wanted to get ready for the new people I was going to meet. High School was considered the fashion club where I lived. I got money from grandma, my mother, my father and even Aunt Jacky coughed up some bread so I could go school shopping. I bought all the latest fads and it was exciting. It helped me to keep myself busy and away from crack.

I tried hard not to think of crack; it took everything out of me to focus my life on preparing for high school. The remaining weeks of the summer were depressing. All I did was stay in the house. I was afraid to be near anyone or be on the streets because it seemed like everything reminded me of crack.

Finally, school started. I was ready to meet school friends; clean and sober friends. I was not ready to give up the weed yet because it helped me forget about the crack. I smoked more weed than ever at that time because I did not want to remember the crack taste, the crack smell and how good I felt when I smoked it. The weed did its job. I was so afraid

I was going to have a hard time forgetting crack; but after one month it was out of sight, out of mind. I did not want to ever relive that horrible night again. That night was enough for me to never want to smoke crack again. It worked.

I started ninth grade and I was so excited to go to school. I thought I would go to Thomas Harding High School and make a positive change in my life. I met so many people my first day, but at the time I did not realize none of them had positive aspirations. I guess it was hard to let go of the bad when you're born and raised around people who did bad things.

I first met a girl named Roni and she became my best friend. I loved her; she was tall like me and light skinned like me. She came from a family that had problems similar to mine. She had an alcoholic, drug addicted mother who abused her physically, verbally and emotionally. Roni would come to school with bruises. I was amazed by that because I think I would have fought back if my mother had ever hit me. Now that I think of it, my mother never hit me. She was never around long enough; but when she was around she never beat me, no matter what I did.

Roni loved everything I loved...nice clothes, having fun and smoking weed. We met the first day of school. She was a sophomore and I was a freshman, but you would have thought it was the other way around. Roni was very poor. I always thought we did bad financially, but I guess you do not appreciate what you have until you meet other folks.

Roni's family lived in a house that was about three hundred years old and the house had a foul odor. Her mother kept the house very dirty and Roni shared her room with her two little sisters. She had to care for her two sisters when her mom would go out. Roni had no other family members she could rely on, so we became very close.

Then there was Barbie, short for Barbara. She was a dust-head, she loved PCP. But she could dress her ass off and that was important to our little crew. Barbie lived in New Jersey with her mother and she stayed with her father on Staten Island when school was in. Her parents were divorced and she was very spoiled. She got anything she wanted. Her father was a big-time dentist who had an office on the ground floor of their house. That is how she got hooked on drugs. At night she would sneak into his dental office and inhale the laughing gas.

Barbie's dad was a workaholic so we basically had the house to ourselves during the weekdays when Barbie was on Staten Island. Barbie came from a good home, well to me and Roni she did. Her mother worked and earned a living. Her mother was drug free and cared a lot about her. Barbie did not like the attention her parents gave her, she hated it. Roni and I could never understand that because we were always yearning for our mothers to love us the way Barbie's parents loved her.

Then there was Sonnie short for Sonia; she hated me but loved Roni. She could not stand me because she was with Roni their entire freshman year and when I came to the school Roni took a liking to me. Roni actually started ignoring Sonnie, and listening to everything I said. Sonnie was the type who had mediocre problems. She never really used drugs; and when she did, she smoked a little pot…never the heavy stuff.

Sonnie's parents were not drug users and she hated when we used drugs all the time. Sonnies' parents were working class poor, they lived in the projects but they only had two kids. They read books to their kids; they went to museums and did real family stuff on the weekends. They even went on family vacations, which Roni and I were jealous of. They were real genuine to their children. They almost appeared perfect.

Sonnie wanted to be with us for only one reason, she wanted to be popular. We became the most popular crew in school. I did not care if Sonnie did not like me; it just made me feel good that she was threatened by me.

The best thing about the crew was that they understood that I had to babysit every day and they would come over to my house and chill with me rather than me going to their homes.

The last and the most important thing about the new set of friends I made, it gained me popularity, something I never had. Because of this I met the cutest guy in the school. This was another reason why Sonnie hated me; she was in love with my new boyfriend Ryan.

Ryan was the best thing that ever happened to me at that time. He was very charismatic, he was handsome and he was street smart, the type girls liked. He showed me how to dress, he bought me jewelry and he never pushed me to have sex with him. We went for long walks and talked about what I liked. He took interest in me and I never experienced that before. No one, not even my family was interested in what I had to say. Ryan cared if I had a cold; he cared if I was sad or overwhelmed and he made me feel like I was somebody. He loved my family and he understood that I had to help raise my aunt's child. Ryan's family loved me and this was the first time I had family outside of my family.

This was the first time I was not teased or felt depressed in a long time. I definitely did not need crack but I needed my weed just to get through the drama that was waiting for me at home. Even though things were good at school, I never knew what to expect when I got home. Either I had to cook dinner, clean the house, or just feed Brandy so she could get ready for bed.

Grandma continued to work nights and I was there in the house watching Brandy alone. Ryan would come by and keep me company if the girls from school were not there. Sometimes if my mother was not in jail she would be there, or if Aunt Jacky got tired of hanging in the streets she would come home for a hot meal and a warm place to rest.

Brandy was getting older and she started to recognize that neither grandma nor I was her mother. She became very angry that her mother would come and go. She would act out by crying at night and when I was at school during the day she would mess the house up. She would rip off her pamper and pee on the floor and once she tore the curtains down. Brandy was suffering from abandonment issues, which led to her acting out.

When Aunt Jacky did come home, she paid little attention to Brandy and I sat there and watched how Brandy was being neglected. I then fell in love with Brandy because what was happening to her had happened to me. I knew exactly what she was feeling; I wanted Brandy not to feel that pain. But there was little I could do because I had my own abandonment issues. I was 15 years old and it was a lot to bear.

By this time Aunt Jacky was seven months pregnant and she continued to use drugs. By now she started stealing from the house on a regular basis when she came to visit. She stole money, clothes and things she could sell, such as VCR's, televisions and anything that was not nailed down. I was tired of her and wanted her to get busted so she could get help. I thought if Aunt Jacky was in jail she could take care of herself and the baby. I knew what Aunt Jacky was going through with her crack addiction. I was only on crack for a short while, but that was enough for me to go through all the stages.

Brandy's father offered on several occasions to take her to Panama for the Christmas Holidays. I always said "no". But this time I decided to call Panama because I felt grandma and I needed a break and Brandy needed to be with her father. Grandma and I were hesitant about sending her but once we committed to it we did not want problems with Brandy's father and his family. They were big time drug dealers and we had to be careful with them.

They lived in Panama and even though Brandy got on everyone's nerves we always wanted to keep Brandy home where we knew she was being cared for. We did not want her in another country where we could not visit her. Brandy was almost two years old and she could talk, so we decided to send her to Panama during the holidays.

Aunt Jacky did not care about Brandy going to Panama. She had no concerns when it came to Brandy. She was glad to get rid other. She got mad when we did tell her that Dexter, Brandy's father called and only asked for Brandy. Aunt Jacky was hurt that Dexter was really over her.

We were in the middle of the school term and I was barely passing my courses. I was into my friends, clothes and new-found boyfriend Ryan. School was not important at the time; I felt I had four years of high school to get my shit together, so why work hard. I enjoyed myself and I was getting attention I never got before at school. I wasn't used to it and it definitely went to my head. The term was about to be over in December for Christmas and I had a couple of weeks to study for my finals. Instead, I was chilling with the gang, smoking weed and talking about our boyfriends.

Ryan and I became best friends, he was nice to me and I did not know what he saw in me to be so nice. This was a tough guy, and everyone at school was afraid of him. But with me, he would talk all night; we would walk, and hold hands which meant so much to me. All the men in my life, up until that time treated me like shit; my father abandoned me and only came around when I begged him for money. The men I knew molested me and treated me like a piece of meat. Ryan was the only one, at that time, who took care of me and I needed that.

Finals were over and I did okay, I passed by the skin of my teeth. I got all C's and I was happy.

Brandy's father came and got her for the Christmas holiday. At first it was scary; we did not want her to go. Her father had not seen her in two years and he and his new wife appeared eager to take her for two weeks.

We did enjoy the peace and quiet in the house. I enjoyed having a life for once; I had forgotten what it was like to be free of children. I had a nice Christmas that year.

My mother was out of prison and Aunt Jacky gave birth to a baby boy who she named Christian. He was born premature, born early due to all the drugs and malnutrition. He was a beautiful baby boy; he had to stay in the hospital during the holidays but Aunt Jacky did not care. She was gone after her two day stay in the hospital and left Christian there. Grandma had to go to the hospital after New Years to pick up Christian since Aunt Jacky abandoned him in the hospital.

Again, my mother showered me and my sister with great expensive gifts for Christmas as she always did when she was not in jail for stealing those gifts. She was with us through New Years. I got to relax and talk with her for a while. Basically the talks were short because, after a while, I could not stand to hear her talk. She was a heroin addict, her voice dragged, and when she talked, every word took forever to come out. Once the scratching started, I was out of there. My mother was a heavy drug user and I was there to witness all of it. She smoked crack, weed, she took uppers, downers and she drank only Remy Martin. But her favorite of all the drugs was the Heroin. She loved to nod, scratch and as she states, "be gone". Her using drugs did not bother me as much as when she left us with grandma. I always knew that even though you become a drug user you can stop; but when you abandon a child, you cannot stop the hurt. And the hurt still goes on in my heart.

Christmas was beautiful, it snowed, I had plenty of nice gifts, and I was surrounded by friends and family. It was a rare moment when my mother was able to come home. She was not there a lot due to the life she chose.

The winter recess was over and it was time for Brandy to return from Panama. School was starting in two days and I was excited that Brandy was coming home; but I also knew it was going to be hard work as well. My mother, of course, had left and went back to her usual self, which was running the streets and hustling to make money. She would send gifts by Aunt Jacky, her beloved sister, or mail gifts to my sister and me. I was ready to return to school. I had missed being with my friends at school, even though I saw them practically every day during the holidays.

Addiction "Aunt Jacky"

Of course, I had to go to the airport to meet Brandy. I really could not wait to see her and I thought she would not remember me. Even though I hated when I had to care for her, I did miss her. I loved my family in spite of the obstacles they put before me. I waited for the plane patiently in the cold dirty terminal. I had to take a taxi to JRB Airport because grandma could not take me since Aunt Jacky had grandma's car. I was becoming impatient at the airport terminal. An announcement was made that Brandy's flight would be late. So, I found a comfortable seat and watched the travelers come in and out of the terminal. It became interesting to me; watching the people coming from different parts of the world. I wondered what their lives were like. I always did that, wondered if everyone had an Aunt Jacky in their family. I finally woke up from watching the travelers when the next announcement came on and stated that the flight arriving from Panama was about to land. I was so excited, I began to get nervous. I do not know why I became nervous but I did. I went in front where she would be coming off the plane.

When Brandy got off the plane she was walking with the flight attendant but I did not recognize her because her father had cut all her hair off. I wanted to cry because she looked like a little boy. This is not the little girl we sent to Panama weeks ago. As soon as she saw me she ran to me and called out my name. She knew exactly who I was and I was so happy to see her. She had gotten taller and she was talking much better than when she left. She kept saying hamburger but saying it like she was originally from Panama. She sounded so cute when she said hamburger. I kept asking her to say the word. The entire train ride home she talked about her stepmother and her siblings that she had met in Panama. She apparently took a liking to Dexter's wife who had treated her well. I was very happy about that. She looked very well fed and well taken care of except for her hair. As soon as I got to the house I called Dexter and asked him what had happen to Brandy's hair and he explained that she did not want anyone to comb her hair so their best solution was to cut it off. Grandma and I were angry with that decision for a long time.

School started and I was back to my old routine. I had gotten my first report card in High School; and I knew if I did not shape up my act, I would be in the ninth grade another year. I could not see the point of trying really hard when no one in my family cared if I went to school or not. None of my friends were doing well in high school, nor was my boyfriend Ryan. Ryan attended school just for show. I soon realized that he never went to class. He came to school every day and was fly, but that was it. Ryan did not care about his education, nor did any of his friends.

We all were in school just to hang out and be somewhere. Every day I would pretend to go to school like I was really going to school. I would make a few classes here and there but I would only pull 60's or 70's. I was not interested in high school for some reason; I had pulled myself out of 6th, 7th, and 8th grade by the grace of God. I had no motivation until the end of the 8th grade and that was because I was dying to get to high school. I was determined to get to high school.

As a freshman in high school, it meant I had four years to get my act together, at least I thought so. It was just a big party for me. I would put on the new clothes my mother stole for me and prance around like I was one of the wealthy kids in school instead of being from a poor family, which we really were. If my mother had not stolen all the clothes I wore, I would have had nothing to wear and I would have been unpopular. That would have killed me because all I had was my popularity going for me at that time and I needed that.

I was introduced to so many new things, things I thought I knew my freshman year. Roni, Sonnie, Barbie and I got closer and closer as the year went on. Barbie insisted on doing PCP and we thought it was a big joke at first. I even tried some once and I will never forget that day. We all ditched school and we were all hanging out at Barbie's house. We were smoking weed and drinking beer. Barbie wanted some angel dust and we were all saying "no" to her. But she insisted on talking about getting some dust. Barbie would go back and forth outside to see if the dealer who sold dust was back on the block; but he was not back from re-up, replenishing his drug supply. So, Sonnie, Roni and I continued to laugh at Barbie and get high off our weed.

Time flew by and we began to get ready to head back home. We always wanted to be home by three o'clock so our parents would not think we did not go to school. Even though most of the time they did not notice or care, but to avoid any stupid questions we preferred to be home on time. Especially me since I had to watch Brandy and Christian as soon as I got home.

Barbie did not get her dust so she was angry. Barbie told Roni and Sonnie she would ride the train with me home since I lived in a different direction from them. Barbie then told me that she wanted to make one stop on the way and I agreed. It was not past my stop, so I was not worried. She made a stop to see a dealer close to my house who sold dust. She copped two charm cigarettes, which are cigarettes dipped in angel dust juice. I thought it was harmless because it was just two cigarettes so I helped her smoke one when she offered. She insisted it was okay; so I did it. I smoked a charm stick. I felt nothing at first and since I was smoking regular cigarettes and weed for so long I thought nothing would happen. While we were smoking the charm stick we were walking back to the train station. Barbie insisted on riding the train home with me, which was only four stops.

As we were entering the train station we were finishing the charm stick. I was just starting to feel the affects of the charm stick when we went through the turnstile and as I was getting on the train. I stood up rather than sitting, even though the train had plenty of seats. I began to feel dizzy and see blurs of things. I felt I was talking in echoes. I asked Barbie if she was okay and she replied she was feeling good.

I started not to remember where I was and I began to panic because I did not sound like myself. I was seeing in 3D and talking in echoes. When I tried to walk toward a seat so I could sit down, I felt like I was walking in slow motion but I knew I was walking normal.

I started to talk loud and my head felt like it was in a big cloud. I tripped out. I asked Barbie to take me to my doorstep rather than leaving me at the train station as we planned. After Barbie agreed to take me home, I lost all consciousness of who I was. She had to take me by my hand and lead me home. I started to cry and shout, "I don't feel good". I could tell Barbie got scared because she was rushing to get me home. She was normal as ever, this was the type of high she loved.

When we finally reached my home, I became more scared. I knew I could not let my grandmother see me like this. Barbie rang the bell to my house and to my surprise my mother answered the door. I was so happy in my dazed mind that my mother came home that afternoon. She knew what to do as soon as she saw me. She asked me what did I take and I told her angel dust. By then, Barbie was gone.

My mother did not lecture me or yell at me; she took me right to the kitchen gave me some ice cold milk and put me to bed. I was glad I had a mother. There are only a few times I ever said that in my life about her. When I awoke she was gone. She left me a note.

I was glad that she left before I woke up because I did not want to explain myself. I knew what I did was wrong and I knew in my heart that I would never touch angel dust again in my life. I began to think about what I did and it became a joke, I laughed so hard. I thought I could handle angel dust just because I smoked crack with my weed and cigarettes. That was one of the worst experiences of my life. I never wanted to use drugs to be unconscious; I wanted to use drugs just to feel good. I always enjoyed being high and understanding what was going on around me. I could not bear the thought of getting high and walking around, not knowing how to conduct myself in public.

Angel dust taught me a lesson; I felt I was above smoking angel dust. I felt I deserved more than a life like that. This was the first time I acknowledged myself as someone. I liked that I made a decision right there at that moment not to smoke dust anymore. I felt I was saving myself for something better. Even though I made the same decision about smoking crack, I felt once again I was being challenged by addiction. It was not easy to give up the crack and it was not easy to come across different drugs on a daily basis and have to fight myself either to not try them or not to try them again.

After I rationalized and committed myself to my decision about the dust I woke up out of that thought and I called Roni and told her what had happened. Roni confessed to me that she had once tried angel dust with Barbie and she too bugged out. She said she was too embarrassed to tell me. Roni stated that she, Barbie and another guy went to the roof of Roni's building once and they were smoking dust and charm cigarettes. Roni stated that she passed out and woke up hours later. Barbie was gone and the guy was there when Roni woke up. The strange thing is when Roni did wake up her pants were open. She believed she was raped. Until this day she is still not sure what really happened. This story never left my mind, even after all these years. I always wondered what happened that day on the roof.

Chapter 3

Finding Myself

It was nearing the end of the school year and once again I had not completed any of my school work. I failed most of my classes. I was becoming more depressed and feeling like I would never get out of high school. The classes I did pass, I only received a 65 or 70 grade. The summer was approaching and I was ready to spend all my days with Ryan and my nights taking care of Brandy and Christian. They both kept me pretty busy at night while grandma worked. By this time, my mother was in prison and now that I think about it, my mother invented the word recidivism; in and out of prison as if it had a revolving door.

My mother was in prison for stealing $30,000 in merchandise but it was comforting because when she was in prison, I did not worry about her. I worried most because of the people she ran with; they were robbers, thieves, drug users, drug sellers, con men and the list goes on. This time, she had to do two years and I had to go to Wedford Hills Prison to see her. I would go once a month and take her a package. I would take food, clothes, weed and dope.

I was 16 years old when she convinced me that it would be okay if I sneaked drugs in a balloon for her. I guess I did it because I loved her very much and at the time I thought it was okay to do. I mean everyone was doing it and especially for family members. It just seemed so normal until one day a friendly visit turned into a possible arrest. I was caught passing drugs to my mother. I had ten bags of dope which is called a bundle on the streets packed in two balloons and then I had

37

one balloon with four dime bags of weed in it. I had them stuffed in my pussy and they went from my pussy to my mothers' pussy which now sounds funny. But once again that was some normal shit to do. Anyway, all together there were three balloons and the only reason I was able to leave the correctional facility was because they searched her after the visit was over and I was already out of the building.

I received a friendly warning by the warden the next morning. He told me if I came back to his prison I would be arrested and they did not have to say it twice. I never visited my mother again after that. That was the greatest and the worse news I ever heard. Before that incident the visits went well. I spent most of my childhood visiting my mother in different prisons. This was the only time I was able to sit with her and talk because she was somewhat patient and sober. I was used to this life, but the visits were depressing to me. I would leave crying every time or I would just stay quiet for hours at a time. It became a norm to go to visit her and in a way I think I felt guilty if I did not go.

I had to visit my mother; that was my mother, that is what you did in my house. No one got punished for their negative actions; you accepted it and moved on.

The summer was just starting and I was too busy to attend summer school. Even though I needed to go, I had planned on being with Ryan and partying with Roni. My grandmother's workload was getting lighter so she was home more in the summer. I was hanging tough with the girls. We would go shopping in the day and buy weed at night. Roni had to work; she worked at a fast food restaurant and this is how she earned her money. Roni's mother Ms. Stone complained all day about Roni working after school. Ms. Stone was a drunk and as soon as you opened her bedroom door it smelled like 151 proof alcohol. But I loved Roni a lot and her mother being an alcoholic did not bother me. Roni had to work to support her and her two little sisters. At my house, my job was cleaning the house and watching the kids. Grandma would give me money for babysitting; she knew it was hard for me. So the money made me feel better.

The summer was going well and I was receiving some support from Aunt Jacky, I guess she knew she had to help out a little since my mother was in prison. She helped babysit her kids when she felt like it; but I knew that at any time she would up and leave or she would end up in prison like my mom.

I thought Ryan and I were getting closer, but we were not. He was getting too old for high school and he made no plans to return to school in the fall. I guess I was in denial because I did not see him distancing himself from me. It was obvious that Ryan and I were growing apart. Even though I cut classes and got high, I wanted more out of life. I just did not know how to do it at that time. I wanted to make up some of the classes I failed, sometime in the future. Ryan just wanted to sell drugs. I thought he would get over that but he felt at 19 years old, with a few high school credits, he would never get out of high school. I knew Ryan was ashamed that he was not going to graduate with the group of kids that he started high school with. Ryan gave up. He could not face the fact that he would be a super senior. I continued to love him because I had faith that he would at least get a job.

Since Ryan was giving me more free time I decided to hang more with Roni. One night Roni, Sonnie, Barbie and I went to the movies and the movie theater was close to Ryan's house. I asked the gang to stop by Ryan's house with me after the movies to surprise him. I never forgot that night because it was so much fun at first.

We all bought some mescaline, tripping tablets that you suck on. The tablet made you laugh for five hours. We went to see a comedy and we were the only fools laughing so loud that the people were yelling at us to shut the fuck up. We laughed at everything. There was a woman who fell and bumped her head while we were in the bathroom and we laughed so hard we were embarrassed.

After the movie we felt great; it was a nice cool summer night. We were strolling down the boulevard and coming towards Ryan's building. I first spotted a young girl who attended the same high school we attended, but we never spoke to each other. Then I spotted Ryan walking behind her, so I stopped so he would not see me.

They began to walk with one another and he kissed her. I was so upset I ran up to them. He was shocked that I stopped at his house unannounced. He tried to introduce us but I was so upset all I could do was yell and scream. She laughed at me like I was an idiot. She slept with my boyfriend that I loved and there was nothing I could do about it. I felt my world was collapsing around me and I wanted to fight her but she was gone before I could raise my fist. So, I lashed out at Ryan. I started to hit and punch Ryan in the face. He did nothing; he just stood there while I beat the shit out of him. I was crying and I was mad but I kept beating on him. I finally got tired and I stopped. I just continued to yell at him. I remember asking, how could he do this to me? I yelled at Ryan, yelling that I took care of him while he was in jail. I had never willingly given myself to anyone but him.

I told him that I thought he loved me. I know it sounds foolish, but I actually believed that shit. I believed he would not leave me. That night Ryan said it was over, he said we did not belong together anymore. He said I should move on because he was not planning on returning back to school. He said he had other plans. I felt cheated and used, even though Ryan was there for me when I needed him most. I was so depressed before I met him.

Those were the best two years I had dating as a teenager. He was my first real love, he made me feel special. He was not like the other guys. Before Ryan, no guy would look at me. I was chubby, pale and I did not have any self-esteem. Ryan gave me confidence, he made me feel pretty, he made other guys notice me that would not have noticed me and they only did so because I was with Ryan. He made me popular in school and that is what scared me the most. I knew it was over between me and Ryan months before we broke up; but I did not want to believe it. I did not want to return to school and be on my own. How could I face everyone, I felt like a loser. Those old feelings came back; I felt no one would notice me and I would not have any friends. Even though I was chubby, when I was with Ryan, he never made me feel that way. He actually made me forget I was chubby.

When we broke up, that is when I realized who I really was. I started to remember when Ryan and I first met; at least one year and some months into the relationship, he was arrested for selling weed. He was sent to a juvenile detention center for 90 days. Not only did I cry for 90 days, I went to see him every weekend. I was devastated; I was having all of my abandonment issues brought back up. I did not realize it at the time, but when he was sent to prison I broke down. I was not myself for the entire time he was in prison. I would only feel good when I got to visit with him. I would come home after the visit and go to bed with one of his shirts. It drove me crazy. I cut my friends off, I smoked even more and I slept more. I felt as if I was getting off a drug, I was addicted to Ryan.

When Ryan's 90 days were coming to an end he told me he wanted me to stop coming to visit him and I thought that was odd because I had been visiting him every weekend. I obeyed his wishes and stopped making visits. He would call me at least twice a week and ask how things were going. He would not tell me the exact date he was going to be released from the detention center. He would just say that he would be home in a couple of weeks.

I went on with my life but I was getting ready for him to come home. I had my hair done, a nice outfit to wear and I just wanted to look good. I was excited about Ryan coming home. He was my life and he took care of me emotionally. I felt something was wrong but I did not want to believe he would do me wrong. I believed in him.

Since I was not visiting Ryan, I decided to call the girls over to my house one evening. Roni, Sonnie and Barbie showed up and we had a party in my bedroom and we started to get fucked up. They were glad to see me since I had cut them off when Ryan got arrested.

We were smoking some weed, Roni was passing something and I was lying on the bed thinking of Ryan. For some reason I kept thinking of him. I then heard someone knock on my bedroom door and it was Ryan laughing. He stopped and looked right into my eyes. He looked so good. I was so fucking happy. The girls welcomed him and they knew to leave so I could be alone with him. Ryan and I talked for a minute and then we tore each other's clothes off. We fucked all night and that was the only time, even now, in my adult life that I ever had the pleasure of being fucked all night. Ryan had a lot of pent up feelings, so it was released on me. I sucked dick willingly for the first time in my life. I was 16 years old and I felt like a grown women that night. We talked during sex, after sex and when the sun was rising. I felt closer to Ryan than I ever thought possible. He really poured out his feelings to me and he made me feel like no man ever did. I never had a father figure and I always wanted a big brother to look over me. Ryan fulfilled all those empty feelings.

But it did happen, he cheated, he was caught and there were two things I could have done. I could have begged him to stay or I could have walked away with dignity. I was 16 years old and I couldn't even spell dignity. I begged him to stay and of course it was a bad scene. He told me he didn't want to see me anymore. He denied he ever fucked that girl who I saw coming out of his home. He kept telling me he is no good for me, he stated I deserved better than him. He confused me because he used psychology on me. He stated he was not planning on returning back to school in the fall. He told me I should get with somebody who is going to do something with their life. Sometimes, until this day I think he knew he was never going to be anything and he saw something in me.

I also think, while he was in jail, he realized he was really gay. But then I thought he was cruel, mean and he used me for my body. I was a virgin to having a relationship before I met Ryan. I felt, for those years he got free pussy and he did not care about me. I felt so stupid, so used, so dirty and alone once again. I could not face any of my friends because I used to brag about how tight me and Ryan's relationship was.

People thought we would last forever. We would go out in public and people thought we were brother and sister, which is how close we were. He became my second half, I grew with him and I fell for him. I did not know what to do but I did know I could not stay depressed. I knew the summer was almost over and school was starting back. It was hard to think about going to school without Ryan. I thought I would not have any friends; I thought people would laugh at me. I was alone, I believed Ryan made me. He was so popular and all the girls liked him. All the guys looked up to him. So what would I be without him? I started to get myself together, accepting phone calls from my friends and I started to get things together in terms of my wardrobe.

I was ignoring Christian and Brandy through those couple of weeks. I was depressed, but I made up for it by spending quality time with them. I took them out and we were a family again. I was glad my grandmother was put on to the credit card scam so I could have more nice clothes for school. She became well educated by my mother.

My grandmother was introduced to the credit card scam and when my mother was in prison grandma would go on shopping sprees. She did this for quite some time. She would work at night and during the day she would go to the department stores and rack up. So I had my order in early so I would be able to at least be fly; especially, if I was not going back to school as Ryan's girlfriend.

Grandma was the provider, no matter what happened to my mother. It was never a second thought when it came to caring for the family. Grandma was the head of the house and that was the one person who would keep this family together. We knew we were not safe when grandma learned how to do the credit card scam. I became very afraid. I was scared she would be arrested like my mom. I hated when she left the house to go shopping. I would feel so much anxiety. My grandmother was an outstanding woman and I could not believe she would actually commit a crime. She went to church and she worked two jobs practically all her life. She was just an honest person but something got to her and until this day I do not know what it was.

Addiction "Aunt Jacky"

What possessed her to do what she did for all those years? I would hear her talk when she was around my mother and Aunt Jacky; she was like a totally different person. She was always preaching to my mom and Aunt Jacky that God was watching them. This made me really believe that what my mom and my grandmother were doing was okay. If grandma is doing it, it must be legal.

I was preparing to be someone new in the fall. I wasted time in high school fucking with Ryan; I wasted time in my life that I could not get back. I got through the summer with the girls getting high, doing dumb shit. Even though I wanted new clothes, I was concerned about my grandmother getting busted. If she was busted that meant no one would be there to care for us; me, Sissy, Brandy and Christian. That thought did not stay in my mind very long. I knew I needed nice clothes and the only way I was going to get them was if grandma would use those credit cards to shop.

Chapter 4

Shit Happens

Aunt Jacky was coming out of jail soon, school was starting in a couple of weeks and I already had my school clothes ready for the New Year.

Aunt Jacky always did less time than my mother. She would get those 90 day sentences and she would be free. That never sat well with me, it always appeared that Aunt Jacky was the snitch. Even though Aunt Jacky came home, she was not better, she was worse. She continued to do the same thing she was doing when she left. She was picked up in a crack raid and spent time in county jail. Anything she could get her hands on was gone and she started to look dirty and spaced out.

She would come out of prison two hundred pounds and a couple of weeks later she would weigh no more than a buck. It was like she came out with a vengeance. She would look at her two children but she would never touch them, she would never kiss them, she would leave them in a blink of an eye. She came home just to sleep, eat and steal.

I was still in the 9th grade but I was 16 years old. I could defend myself if she started with me. But she never wanted to fight, she just wanted her way and that's how shit went down. It was either her way or the highway in the house. She was grandma's baby, she controlled the house. Whatever Aunt Jacky said, that is the way shit went down. Even until this day, if Aunt Jacky tells grandma the sky is black, grandma would be on her knees praying to God to keep the sky blue and white. I always believed until today that Aunt Jacky had something on grandma and no one knew. I thought there is no way anybody could

Addiction "Aunt Jacky"

love Aunt Jacky. I think God had to step away from this one.

The shit Aunt Jacky did to grandma is unbelievable. She stole her rent checks, she stole numerous cars from grandma, she jumped bail, grandma lost her home and she even dropped her children on grandma. Grandma never said anything. The part that really killed me was the children part. How could anyone leave their children? Especially after their older sister did it and Aunt Jacky witnessed how much my sister and I suffered when my parents took off. She saw what we went through, how hard it was for us. I always thought she would learn from that, but instead she followed my mother's negative ways.

Aunt Jacky was gone again and I was stuck with the kids and it became routine by the time I was 16. Although I was hurt, I took care of them. I do not remember getting upset about the kids any more, it became a norm. I was just unhappy about myself. My family problems did not beat me; the school part was beating me. I already knew that Aunt Jacky was shit; I already knew that my mom was a prisoner for the rest of her life, even if she got out. She's been in prison too much of her life to get it together. I always wanted her to be a mother, even now. I had to come to terms with the fact that she loved the street game. I saw my mom shoot heroin. I think I lost all respect for her then; I loved her so much. I was caught between love and hate for her. But I remained loyal to her.

For some reason, at the age of 16 I knew I could not afford to live on my own; but I knew I had to depend on myself for everything. That is when I realized if I do not start getting my shit together I will be nothing.

Things were going well and I was preparing to go back to school and I was nervous because of the Ryan thing. I thought I would not get any respect from my peers. I even noticed how one of my friends treated me. Sonnie was glad Ryan and I were over. She told the entire school Ryan dumped me for another girl. But I was strong; I held my head up high and rocked every new outfit my grandmother stole for me. But little did I know; no one cared if Ryan and I were not together; it wasn't about Ryan it was about me. They liked me, they wanted to know me. That was so important to me, I survived.

I even started going to class that year. I became known to the teachers in a positive way, for the first time in my life. I actually liked that feeling, but I was so far behind it would have taken a miracle for me to get out of high school on time. I was supposed to be in the 11th grade but I was still in the 9th grade. This made me want to go back to cutting; I started to feel like, what's the use, especially since my friends were not supportive.

I was always reminded by the teachers who knew I was two years behind that I had a lot of work to do to catch up. Although I was going to class, none of my friends went to class. I was still the outsider when it came to wanting to get my education. This was the first time I felt pulled by peer pressure. I wanted to go to class but my friends would say we are not graduating so what is the point.

But I did have someone who believed in me, even though they did not. There was one teacher who believed in me, she was my reading teacher. She would give me my assignments to do at home because she knew I was not always going to be in class. She saw something in me; she would ask me to go to the store to get her bagels after my class work was finished. She knew I wanted to get outside to meet my friends and that was the only way I would be able to get outside once I was in the building. She would give me a store pass and I would see my friends, smoke some weed and come back to class. My friends did not understand my teacher; they would say she trusts you. That is when I realized she did trust me; that made me feel great. That is when I realized that people will respect me if I respected myself.

It was that school year when grandma told me we were moving back to Brooklyn, I thought that was the miracle I was looking for. I did not know it then, but it was the best thing that ever happened to me. I did not know what to think, I was afraid of the unknown; but I did know I wanted to go to a new school and start fresh. The fall semester was ending and I was pulling all 65's and I loved it. It was the first time I passed all my classes in high school. I was looking forward to going back to Brooklyn; I was actually calling up old friends who I had left in the 6th grade. I could not believe I was living in Staten Island all those years. I was 12 years old going on 13 when I moved to Staten Island. I knew what it was like to live in Brooklyn and I could not wait to get back to the tranquility, the brownstones, the tree lined blocks and all the culture Staten Island lacked.

I knew I was going to miss my friends, especially Roni and Barbie. Barbie was dying out; she was beginning to use dust every day. She was moving in slow motion and she became a dust-head. She became distant from the group. She stopped coming to school, she stopped dressing nice and she was defiant to her mother. It was as if she didn't care anymore. It seemed she was tired of pretending and she wanted to be herself...a dust-head.

The one thing we did learn was that we all had changed. Roni decided to get her diploma and since she was so far behind she dropped out and got her GED. No one could say anything because she was older than me and she did get her GED diploma. She was proud because her mom was a drunk and she too had nothing to live for. Sometimes I thought her situation was worse because she had nothing. The stuff she did have she had to work after school for it. Nothing was wrong with that, but it wasn't for me. I mean, my job after school was taking care of the kids and I was rewarded by getting new clothes and getting money.

Roni and I decided we were going to be the best of friends after I moved, she stated Barbie is gone now and it was just us. Sonnie was going to graduate, she always went to class and she had plans to attend college. Sonnie broke off from the group, she got what she wanted and that was popularity.

Roni surprised her family when she passed the GED. She wanted to move away from her mother. She was tired of being nothing; she realized that once I left she was going to be alone. It was a good thing that we separated because we were more damage to one another together than apart. One thing we noticed was that no one wanted to make the other look stupid, meaning it was hard for all of us to say we needed help. We needed to get out of high school. I do not know why one of us could not have told each other we were acting like assholes. We all wasted two and a half years of our life getting high and flunking school and no one said anything.

Roni was in high school one year ahead of me so she should have graduated a year before me. Roni looked at me and a sad look came upon her face. I felt her loneliness. I knew it would be hard for her because she had no friends other than Barbie and me. The girls in her neighborhood hated her and her cousins who lived in New Jersey were fly girls who just did not accept her. So, I promised I would keep in touch with her when I relocated back to Brooklyn. I knew she was going to be alright even though her mother, Ms. Stone was an alcoholic and a heavy drug user.

So, we were all packed, ready to go. The deal was done on the house and we were heading back to Brooklyn. I was so fucking happy. We had the moving truck packed with all our shit. Even Roni came and spent the first two nights with me. We had a lot of unpacking to do; this was challenging because my mother and Aunt Jacky was not around. I had to do all the unpacking myself.

First I started with the upstairs. I cleaned the bathroom, I cleaned grandma's room and she got settled in quick. I then began to clean the living room and kitchen; this was a task but it had to be organized for everyone to be comfortable. The brownstone was nice; it was on a tree-lined block with grass and friendly black people, working class people. I felt right at home.

Grandma was getting too old to work so she was asked to retire from her job. This was hard for her because she worked at the hospital for more than 30 years. She just retired from her second job a few years ago when we were in Staten Island. She always talked about that job; she worked for very nice Jewish people in a book binding company. She used to come home with this rubber protector for her thumb and it always made me wonder what she did at that job to have to wear a rubber thumb protector. She used to say, "I do not want to get a paper cut so I have to protect my fingers". She worked at the book binding company for over thirty years and she retired because they had closed down. So, when Mellow Brook also asked her to retire she was hurt. She only knew how to work hard and she worked all her life. I could not imagine today working two jobs for over thirty years. She was 65 years old and she was not ready to retire. She was strong, active and willing to put in eight hours wherever she could.

She went on to retire and she was thankful that she had my little brother, who was handicapped, to take care of. I haven't talked about him because it takes me time to introduce him. He suffered the most. His nickname was Little Man and he was not supposed to live past age two; he made it to twelve years old. He was born with all kinds of abnormalities. My mother used many drugs while pregnant with him. I had to watch him at night for many years. He was the worst to care for because he suffered like an animal.

My grandmother would provide adequate care for him. At first, she had a sitter in the day helping out while we kids were at school. But at night when she went to her night job at Mellow Brook she would leave him with us kids and my Aunt Jacky who came home when she wanted to or when she was not in jail. It was hard to find a night sitter; she felt me and my sister were old enough to care for him if Aunt Jacky left the house.

I started watching him when I was 11 years old. But it felt like forever. He took Phenobarbital, a drug to minimize seizures; at least 3 times a day and he only ate mashed food. All he could do was lie in the bed for twelve fucking years. He could not walk, he could not talk, he was a vegetable, why was he ALIVE. He could not tell us when he was hungry, we guessed. Things are so different now and because of medical advancements his life would have been easier. I could not imagine today having my little brother in the house incapacitated. I loved him so much; he hurt my heart every time I looked at him. I did not know what to do anymore; I hated caring for him because it made me so depressed and guilty.

This boy did not know why he was here, all he knew was that he had bed sores and ribs sticking out of his stomach because he would never gain weight no matter what was mashed up and given to him. My grandmother loved him so much; she would feed him from her mouth. She would chew food up and give it to him.

So when she retired she knew she could devote her time to him. She stayed home all day and all night with him. She went out with him and this was the first time she could express how she really felt about him. She got him enrolled in school and she got him a new wheel chair so he could sit up during the day. He was thriving for once in his life. He was never able to talk or show any feelings but she communicated with him. She made up a name for him when he was born; it was "Little Man". She named him that because when he was born he had the face of a grown man.

Little Man was very cute. He had long pretty eye lashes, a caramel complexion, flawless skin and he had long wavy hair that the family would braid. Grandma dressed him in the best clothes, he looked good going to school and I felt proud for the first time to have a brother. This was important to me because when I was 8 years old I was embarrassed of him. When my friends came over I used to hide him. Their brothers were normal and mine was handicapped. Even at an early age I knew why he was fucked up. My mother used heroin when she was pregnant with him. Now I understand why grandma got him, she had to go and get him because they would not release him to my mother from St. Kings Hospital.

My mother shot heroin rather than sniffing it back then, it was more potent that way. He was exposed to her malnutrition, her illegal drug use, her non prenatal care and her hanging out at night without sleeping.

Addiction "Aunt Jacky"

I remember seeing her one morning thinking she was going through morning sickness, she looked horrible. I can truly say that she was not going through morning sickness, she wanted her medicine. She called heroin her medicine. She was having withdrawal not morning sickness. Anyone who ever saw a heroin addict withdraw knows what that symptoms is shaking, trembling, sweating and vomiting. It is not a pretty sight I know my brother suffered as much in her stomach as in his life.

Everyone was doing fine. Little Man was in school, Brandy and Christian were getting older and learning to feed themselves. Brandy was turning four years old and Christian was turning two. Grandma was more helpful to me when it came to babysitting, since she did not have to work. She would even get up and make dinner. But this would not last long.

Aunt Jacky could never stay away too long. She wanted grandma to commit crimes with her; I believe she felt less guilty about her own mistakes if she took her mother with her to shop with stolen credit cards. I know for sure that my mother and Aunt Jacky taught my grandmother the credit card scam and they were professionals. They needed a sweet old women character to ride with them when they went into those stores. They told my grandmother it was a sweet deal and she would never get caught. They promised her things she never could get after working 30 years on two jobs. It was hard for grandma to turn them down. She had it hard all her life and she struggled to raise her seven children on her own when her husband died young. She was left alone.

Grandma began to go shopping with my mother and Aunt Jacky. She was the little old lady and no sales person would ever suspect her of credit card fraud. They would get VCR's, TV's, Camcorder's, Computers and sell them to the ARABS downtown. They would get top dollar for their merchandise. On top of that, I would get top of the line clothes. I got fur coats at 16 years old. I had designer name bags. All my friends were jealous and I fit right into the dress code of Brooklyn.

I was happy in my new home and my new school, Morgan Jackson High School; especially since they gave me a sweet deal. I thought no one cared until I got to MJ. The principal sat down with me and told me that they would put me in the 11th grade, the grade I belonged in if I took school seriously. They knew I was fucked up from looking at my transcripts. They told me to take night school classes. If I succeeded that semester I would be able to graduate within the following year. I took the deal and ran all the way home. I was excited; I knew I could do it. I could not believe they believed I could do it. I told myself if they are willing to give me a chance, I should take it. In reality when I did tell my friends and family, it was not news for them. They knew I had potential. I had to make the decision on my own. I began to work hard and go to all my classes and I found it was so easy. I could not believe I missed out on those years of school for nothing. I missed out on the school activities; I was in a school play at MJ. I played Harry in the play, Guys and Dolls. I have a deep voice so I played the part well. I was proud of myself, even though no one came to see me in the play.

Grandma's scam was going well. She was making money and she was getting over. Aunt Jacky was in and out of the house as usual but this time it was a good thing because I could not stand her ass by this time. She treated her kids like shit and she did not care what they were doing. She did not care that she missed Christian's first walk and his first sound. She did not care that Brandy still peed in the bed because she missed her mother and father. Brandy cried at night for someone to love her. I was abandoned by my mother and that cry was so familiar. My mother also chose her lifestyle over me and I could never understand that. I used to ask her, "When are you coming home"? I think that is a fucked up question to have to ask a parent. Brandy and Christian's pain was so vivid to me and I understood their misery and this made me angrier. This made me hate Aunt Jacky and I wondered why no one else hated her.

Aunt Jacky was really losing it; she was selling things as fast as she could steal them to support her drug habit. I remembered once how I adored Aunt Jacky and how I would do anything for her, but she has done so much wrong it was impossible to forgive her.

Although I was young, I felt the anguish those kids were going through. I was young but I knew that I had to mature quicker than my peers because I was abandoned by my parents as a child. That puts age on you because you become bitter about not having parents at an early age. I worried about things as a child when I should have been doing childlike things. I missed out on my childhood waiting for my parents to appear. I wanted to do what regular kids did with their parents. Instead I was raising kids and being a parent.

Spring semester at MJ went very well, I was pulling good grades and I was motivated. I became popular overnight but not for my clothes, for the first time for my efforts. I had all the teachers in my pocket and it was because I was their success story. They gave me a chance that I should have blown according to my past but I took that chance and made a success of it. I was even actually considering going to college. I knew I was not college material because none of the women in my family ever earned a college degree. Grandma did go to nursing school and obtained her LPN but it was not a four year college degree. This was the first time I saw myself as being okay. I felt like I could possibly be somebody.

Even though I was popular and doing well in school which kept me going, I still felt like shit on the inside, on most occasions. I never felt good inside, I believe that this is so because I always held everything in. I do not remember once ever expressing how I felt about raising the kids, having a drug addicted mother, having a father as a molester and the guilt I felt when I used drugs.

Chapter 5

Dealing

I met a girl at MJ named Michelle Black and she was real. This was the first friend I ever met who did not do drugs, she did not curse and she was not a smoker. I never had a friend like her before. Michelle was not stupid; she knew the streets even though she did not do drugs. Her mother and father lived together and they were big heroin addicts and that is what Michelle and I had most in common. Michelle hated drugs because it took her parents away from her.

Although her parents were on heroin they were deeply in love. They were married in the 60's and Michelle was their only child. Michelle's parents had a beautiful home left to them by Michelle's grandmother. So, since the house was paid for, Michelle's mother did not work, she received welfare and her father hustled side jobs. I was very impressed with Michelle's parents, even though they were on drugs. The drug part actually did not bother me as much as it did Michelle. It really affected her. I was impressed by their love for one another and for living so many years together in one home as a family raising their daughter despite their heroin addiction. They kept a lovely home and it just amazed me. Michelle was like me, she knew what it was like to have a mother on drugs. We would compare horror stories about our mother's drug use without having to feel ashamed. That was our way of getting the shit off our chest.

Michelle was very sober and clean. She wanted to be the opposite of her parents. She lived several blocks from me, but she was within walking distance from my house. Michelle had this knack for cheering me up when I was depressed. I would smoke weed every day and she would say nothing. She wanted to be around me because she needed to be around someone who understood what she was going through. I understood her, I understood how she felt.

We became a team at MJ. Michelle was having some problems with her grades but it seemed like when I got there she started to do extremely well. I was in the 11th grade and she was in the 12th grade. She and I dreamed of getting our own apartment together. We thought we would be good roommates. One night Michelle and I were baking brownies and of course, I was smoking weed and she broke down. She cried about the fact that she witnessed her parents getting high all the time. She stated she used to watch her parents shoot each other up with heroin at breakfast and dinner like clock work. She said when her grandmother died she was 5 years old and that is when her parents inherited the home. Michelle explained that is when she noticed her parents sticking needles in their arms. Her worst nightmare was when they both passed out after shooting each other up. Michelle said she was 10 years old and both her parents were passed out at the kitchen table. She said she must have shaken them all night before they awoke to her crying. Michelle was traumatized from that moment on and that was why she could not take drugs herself. I thought to myself wow, Michelle had to be afraid thinking her parents were dead all night. For the first time I started to think my life was not so bad. This made Michelle so depressed that she did not want to go home at times and she would chill at my house. She thought my problems were easier to deal with. I thought differently. I wished I only had a drug addicted mother to deal with. I had two to three kids to take care of, at any given time, and a drug addicted mother.

Michelle was an only child. She did not have anyone to care for and I was jealous of that. I was jealous of how she coped with her problems because she did not smoke weed to deal with her problems. Michelle dealt with her problems by eating her favorite desert which was butter pecan ice cream. She would get depressed and eat ice cream all day and all night. We were real different; I would smoke trees all day and all night when I got depressed. I admired her because she beat the odds, she was high risk to use drugs and she did not.

Michelle realized she did not have enough credits to graduate. She learned she would have to complete 6 more credits in order to have her gym credits she would need to graduate in June. She was not angry with the situation, she was actually happy because she just wanted to graduate from high school. When I got there Michelle was finishing up the 11th grade, going into 12th grade. She went to night school and morning school which brought her grades up. She did make it to the 12th grade. I felt proud of myself because even through all the drugs and depression I made it to the 12th grade and I had a good chance to graduate from high school on time.

I decided to call Roni and share my thoughts as we did once in a while since my move to Brooklyn. Roni was surprised to hear from me and as she talked she reminded me of a time when I used to get sick and I would have difficulty breathing. I was going back and forth to the hospital. They diagnosed me with asthma. I had to carry the pump everywhere I went and it interfered with my social life. I hated it. No one took it seriously; I only took it seriously when I was very ill. It got so bad that I had to get an air conditioner put in my room. This is one of the reasons I wanted to forget Staten Island.

However, Roni and I continued to talk even though I was reminiscing about my illness. We stayed on the phone and talked to one another to catch up on old times. Roni and I did admit that day that the traveling became too much and this is one of the reasons we have not visited one another as often as we did in the past.

One day I called Roni and she told me she suspected her mother of doing more than drinking; she believed her mother was smoking crack heavily. Roni sounded more mature than before, like she had more responsibility. She also sounded like things had gotten worse at home; I knew that sound. I understood what Roni was going through. I explained to her that things were getting tight on my end and that things were changing for me too. I let her know that grandma was not as fast as my mother and Aunt Jacky; and grandma could not steal the clothes as fast as them. I was used to getting new clothes every day, now it was every other month or so. Also, when grandma went shopping I had to go with her because she did not know how to pick my clothes. So that limited me from getting new clothes because I was too chicken to go into any store on a regular basis. I would get nervous just thinking about going to the stores. I would freak out and become obvious and that could have gotten everyone busted. By this time, my morals started to change. I was not as interested in new clothes as I was before. Don't get me wrong, I wanted nice clothes, but I started to understand the risk. I felt like my life was more important than shoplifting for clothes. I became more involved in school and my family. I was not as interested in the hanging out as I did when I lived in Staten Island. I gained weight; I felt unattractive, which was okay for me at that time. I needed and wanted to focus on my education for the first time.

I had the opportunity to have a relationship with a boy named Sean Comrie, a rival of Ryan's from Thomas Harding high school in Staten Island. I would use Sean for sex and little conversation, he did both terribly. But how could I complain, I was fat and Ryan hated him so that made me happy to know he was miserable knowing I was fucking his enemy. Ryan was cuter, always the best dressed and most popular. Ryan was everything. When Ryan broke up with me, I turned to Sean. The Sean thing did not last long, he was boring and he dressed like a nerd. As soon as we moved to Brooklyn, I knew he was just a fling, he was just for sex and that was not good because I had no love for him. I was used to having sex when I was in love, not just having sex for nothing. I did not have any feelings for Sean, yet with Ryan I loved him very much and the sex was pleasurable. I did not have many opportunities to break up with too many guys when I was 17 years old, but I was able to break up with Sean and it felt good.

The kids were doing well; Brandy was about to start school and Christian was in diapers. They were very hyperactive kids. They broke everything that was not nailed down or broken already. It was hard raising them because I did not understand their behavior. It made me furious that they broke my belongings. I hated them at times; I had to put a lock on my bedroom door. Although Brandy had me and grandma, she suffered a lot as a child. Grandma only knew how to love; she did not know how to care for Brandy. Grandma worked all her life and even though she had children she could not raise them properly because someone had to feed them. She was just there to clean, cook and wash clothes for them. The same goes for me, I loved the kids so much but I did not know how to care for the kids as they should have been cared for. Brandy's hair was never combed right; she wet the bed so she stunk at times and she never had proper dental work done. The house never really stayed clean because grandma was getting older and it was hard for her to do house work. I took no interest in cleaning, I was a teenager and my plate was already full. Grandma would leave glasses in her room, dishes in the sink and dirty clothes would sit for days. My sister and I would clean as much as we could but it was too much for us to handle.

We lived in a house with three kids and two teenagers. We had traffic because of the people grandma and Aunt Jacky allowed to come into our home. My mom would come in and out, Aunt Jacky and her friends would come in and out and our famous uncle Bart, Aunt Jacky's brother. It is funny now how I look at my mother's brothers and sisters. They all were fucked up losers at one point in time. I always blamed them for being who they were. How can so many losers come out of a sweet woman who believed deeply in God? My grandmother bore all these losers but she was the type of woman who fed the homeless, gave shelter to the needy and took care of the handicap for 30 years. She was the type of woman who would bring the mentally ill kids home for the holidays from Mellow Brook and buy them all sorts of gifts. She has been drug free all her life while working not one job but two jobs for thirty-eight years. How could she bear seven greedy, conniving, drug addicted, mean-spirited children? What did she do in her life to have such bad luck with her children?

Addiction "Aunt Jacky"

Her oldest boy killed a man when he was 25 years old. He served 30 years in prison and was killed the day he was supposed to be released from prison by some gang member. My family still believes it was payback from the murder he committed all those years before. He was never supposed to have been released but he was pardoned and was given a second chance for good behavior in prison. Her second son was such a large man, a big time drug user and seller; he was known to the FBI as "round man". Once, the FBI came to my house when I was a child and surrounded the house. I mean this was some serious shit. We called him "candi" and on that day he dressed up in my grandmother's wig and makeup and walked right out the front door. They did not know who he was; they must have guessed he had a twin sister. Every time I imagined him in that dress I got so scared because I thought he would be shot. He finally got caught, did 20 years for murder, drug trafficking and he died in 1989, in prison. He was another one buried on jail soil; no one knew he was dead until two weeks later.

The third son was an army man; the army drove him away from his kids and his mother. He died in a car accident in 1992. I loved him, he was kind and gentle to me and my sister. But the Army caused him to have some mental problems. He married a mean woman who my family hated and they relocated to California where he died.

Her fourth son almost made it. He graduated high school with good grades, he was accepted to a University to fulfill a football scholarship and he played there until he was recruited to play for a team in Philly. He played in Philly for three years. He then had a knee injury and became dependent on pain killers that led to crack cocaine. He fell in love with the white powder.

Now for her two daughters, the oldest being my mother, who never in her life had a real job and if she did it was not in my lifetime. Since I was able to walk and talk "my mommy dearest" never took responsibility for her life. Either she hustled or leaned on a man. She never leaned on the family for support unless she needed to be bailed out of jail. When she became tired of that she relied on her street game.

Dealing

She sold drugs; she used the credit card scam so much that she was wanted in different states for that alone. My mother forever is a loser for leaving her children. Don't get me wrong, she made sure my sister and I had everything we needed, private schools growing up, the best of clothes, restaurants, Broadway plays and freedom. But she never took time to see how my sister and I were really. She just saw the surface but not what we were feeling inside. We never had a real mother and daughter talk and I feel I missed so much. This to me was worse than the crimes she committed.

Then there was Aunt Jacky, she was the worst of the worst. She started out young with her crime waves; she abused not just herself but her family. She was hard; at least her brothers and sisters were nice to the family when they were around. At times they were pleasant to be around but not Aunt Jacky, she was hateful. She would steal your stuff and say "what you going to do about it"? All you could do was cry. She had no feelings about anything and that made you scared of her. People on the streets observed this behavior and that is how she became known on the streets. Everyone knew if she did not have it, she would take it.

My grandmother had seven children but I only named six, just because the seventh child abandoned the family once he realized his brothers and sisters were losers. His name was Uncle Fred. He needs his own introduction because I hate him for different reasons. He was the one who made it; he had a beautiful home. He never touched drugs, nor did he steal for a living. He has a successful career in business. My sister and I loved going to his home. He had guest rooms for everyone to sleep in and his house was like something out of a magazine. He had a pool in his backyard; he had a swing set, seesaw and grass that smelled sweet. I would just lie in the grass and take deep breaths while getting a tan.

The house was clean and bright, it was well furnished and it had a pool table in the basement where there was a big screen TV for guests. I admired him, loved him and I wanted him to be my dad instead of my uncle. He acted like he loved us. Thanksgiving was the day for the family because he would host the dinner at his home. It was a festival to me because his home was my castle. The neighbors were white and friendly. He kept so much food in his house you thought he owned a market. Every time my sister and I were there, we would have snacks for days. This is the home where I was inspired. I thought of endless possibilities, I thought I could fly when I was at his home. His home was perfect and I think he knew how my sister and I felt when we were able to visit his home. We were so happy.

One day grandma called everyone into the living room and stated Uncle Fred was moving to Jacksonville, Florida and he was selling his house. I cried for days. He was the one who helped keep the kids on a level of saneness, we believed in him. He was our savior on holidays and weekends. I knew things would change when he left and they did. I felt abandoned all over again. I knew why he left and I believe he wanted to disassociate himself from the family. He was embarrassed by us. I knew this; I knew he got tired of holding the family together. He got tired of the family asking him to bail them out of jail; he got tired of his siblings getting busted. I know he was tired, I was tired and I was a teenager. He packed everything, sold the house and was gone. Things did change for the worst; we had nobody to go to on holidays. We had no one else good enough in the family to run to. I never forgave him because since he left he never visited us and it has been about 30 years since he left. I have not seen Uncle Fred in over 30 years. He has not seen his mother and siblings for over 30 years. He used to call once a year and that was usually on mother's day and those calls stopped coming.

Chapter 6

The Bust

The school term was over and I did well, I pulled an eighty average and I was happy. I was amazed that I did that well. Although I did well, my counselor pulled me into his office to discuss college and I turned to him and said I was just trying to get out of high school. I cannot possibly think of college. The truth was that I was scared as shit, I thought if I did get out of high school that was enough. I never thought beyond high school. I was afraid of college, a person like me does not, I thought, go to college. I honestly thought I would fail and if I did apply for college; no school in their right mind would accept me, so why try.

Anyway, we had a couple of weeks off for the Christmas holiday and I planned to relax those two weeks. But my grandmother had something else planned for me. After school that evening, Michelle and I decided to go straight to my house because I had to check on grandma and the kids but what I found when I got home was my worst nightmare. My sister who was one year younger than me was sitting on the floor crying, the kids were sleeping and Little Man was in school. I thought maybe she broke up with one of her boyfriends, she had so many. But her cry was different; she said the words I dreaded all my life. GRANDMA GOT BUSTED. I was so scared, I did not know who to call, Aunt Jacky was with her and my mother was serving time in Wedford Hills. So we got ourselves together and started to clean the house. Michelle helped us; we all were very quiet while we cleaned. It was like we were in shock. Michelle helped cook food for the kids and fed them. She met the bus that dropped off Little Man and laid him in his bed.

The phone rang, it was the officer from the precinct that grandma and Aunt Jacky were being held at. The officer explained to my sister that they had to see a judge and it would take hours before they would get to see one. He then explained what they were being charged for; we knew what they were being charged for. The officer stated that grandma was arrested for credit card fraud and grand larceny. Aunt Jacky had a warrant for her arrest for another case but grandma's record was clean. So, she had a good chance of getting out that night. But we were still worried; this was an eye opener for me and my sister. Right then and there we knew we had to get our lives together because we would be on our own soon. That was hard to imagine, we never had real role models who moved out on their own and made it. That made us scared because we did not witness our older family members live on their own. They all lived with grandma one way or another; they never had their own home or even an apartment. If they did rent a room or an apartment it wouldn't be long before they would be back at grandma's house.

My sister became affected by grandma's incident with the police. At the time, grandma was 66 years old. We believed she was the strongest in the house and she was. We thought nothing could happen to her.

Several hours later, we finally received a call from grandma telling us she was on her way home and to not worry, but we did. Aunt Jacky had to serve time for a warrant she had in a previous case. She had to serve 15 months this time and by the time she got out my mother would be home. Grandma was glad to be home. She took a bath, she kissed the kids and she said nothing of her encounter with the police. Even though grandma was released, my sister and I were more afraid than my grandmother.

The next day I heard grandma on the phone telling the person who sold the checks and credit cards to her that they were bad checks. She thought he stole them the day he sold them to her, but apparently the guy had them for a week and the owner of the checks and credit cards had already reported them stolen. The credit card bank game is called jostling. This is when the jostler goes into an establishment and steals someone's wallet, purse or credit card. After the jostler has these items he/she would either sell them or use them themselves. But the secret is to use them as soon as you get them because half the time the owner does not know their shit is missing until days later. Apparently in Aunt Jacky and grandma's case the person who sold them the checks and credit cards used them prior to giving them to grandma or they sat on them and time caught up with them. Either way it was an eye opener for all of us.

This did not scare grandma. As matter of fact, it actually made her tougher. She had her own connection. Even with Aunt Jacky behind bars she willingly wanted to go to the stores. I always thought that Aunt Jacky and my mother influenced her, but it turned out she loved it as much as they did. She was back on the streets before you knew it. This time she was alone and I was more afraid of her getting busted again. She thought she knew the streets but she did not. She had men coming over to our home selling her checks and credit cards and they looked high and broke. They looked desperate to sell their work but I knew Grandma was naive and did not know whether they could be trusted.

Once we were in Five Town Mall shopping for shoes and grandma would buy us ten pairs at a time so we did not have to come back. She went to the register and she paid with the credit cards she bought the night before. She waited to sign the receipt and it took longer than she expected. Of course, I started freaking out and started walking around the store. The store manager started asking a lot of questions and told the security guard to lock the doors. They did and they called the bank the credit card came from to verify the owner of the credit card. But the banks were closed, the manager looked at grandma and said have a nice day ma'am. We flew out of there and never returned to that store for nothing.

This was the last straw for my sister; she was overwhelmed by my grandmother's greed. She was tired of the kids and she met a Chinese guy mixed with Polish and his name was Gabriel Chan. Even though Sissy was there in the same house, she escaped emotionally. She was one year younger than I and she and grandma did not like each other. My sister never discussed her personal relations with me but I knew she was fucking him. She was 16 years old and she was cutting classes to be with him.

By the time we got to Brooklyn she had to travel from Brooklyn to Staten Island to go to school. She did not transfer schools like I did when we moved. It seemed like she just gave up. I could not believe she would leave school like that. I still don't know if it was the pressure of the problems going on in the house or because she fell in love with the Chinese guy and saw a way out. Her attitude became vain and harsh towards my grandmother. My sister and she would fight for every little thing. My sister's tone became violent when speaking to grandma and that is when my sister decided she had to go. My grandmother pushed her out when she told her she was a loser and she would never amount to nothing. I always thought that was a cliché but it stuck with my Sissy and made her feel so bad that I think she's unemployed right now because of those words. My sister knew she was leaving school long before we knew about her dropping out and that was what that fight was about. That was the last fight my grandmother had with my sister in that house.

My sister left the house the night of the big fight with grandma. I woke up the next morning to put up the Christmas decorations and the Christmas tree to an empty bed next to mine. I thought Sissy decided to go make breakfast or start decorating before me. When I did not see Sissy I ran to the closet and all her clothes were gone. I was devastated, I could not talk. I just stood there and thought *I am alone; I am alone with all this shit to worry about.* I suddenly forgot about the Christmas decorations and started to think about how my sister and I were not close in a hang out way but we were connected emotionally. She was there when I cried all night for my mother; she was there with me through the visits to see my mother. What would Christmas be without her? She opened her Christmas gifts with me for 17 years. Who would be there for me when I got scared? I always thought we had each other's back; we fought a lot because we were angry at my mother and father. We never got along but we were close because we had to be. I believe the reason we fought was because she looked like my mother and I looked like my father. We reminded each other of the people who abandoned us. Until this day we cannot be in the same room together too long without arguing. But I love her very much.

When I woke up out of the shock, I went to grandma's room to explain that my Sissy was gone. That was the nickname I gave my sister. Grandma told me something that day I will never forget. She said "I know" and "I am glad that bitch left because she will never amount to nothing anyway". I was confused, sad and felt abandoned all over again. I know grandma was angry but she loved me and my Sissy. I realized that grandma had so much on her plate that her attitude about family by this time was either you're in or you're out. She was not concerned about how we felt because she never considered the life we were living as dysfunctional or unpleasant. Grandma hid that very well. She acted like things were the way they should be but I knew and my sister knew that our life was not normal.

Grandma acted cool and calm about my sister's disappearance and I played the part that way as well. I was missing my Sissy. I eventually found out where she had moved to, but at the time I was too angry to talk with her. I did not want to speak to Sissy ever again. I felt she was not my sister anymore. I could not bear to think she was free from the bullshit and she left me to deal with it by myself. I always thought we would get out together. I knew it was hard living with my family. I was going through it too, but I did not bail out on my family. I hated what my family believed in. I hated living in fear and I hated not having parents who cared for their children but I had to swallow all that shit and help my family.

They say children who are born in alcoholic households become the supporter of the family; they become the caretaker of the family because that is what they had to do as children. Even though my mother was not an alcoholic, she had abandoned us and that automatically gave me the authority to become the caretaker. My sister was too weak. I, at that moment, realized I was chosen to be the next in charge. The loneliness kicked right in and the burden on my shoulders felt heavier. The family was in my hands at 17 years old. I cleaned, cooked, watched the kids went to school and worried most of the time.

At times, I wanted to call my sister but she moved far away. She moved to San Francisco. I could not call her and when she called it always seemed like I was angry. Our talks were short and brief.

I got through the Christmas holidays alone, I was depressed; Mommy was in jail, Aunt Jacky was in jail and grandma was bitter. Grandma could not understand what went wrong. She raised my sister and I and she thought we would all be together. I could tell the hurt was kicking in. My sister was only 16 years old when she left and she did not leave on a good note. We had to move on. Grandma and I had to stick together. In a lot of ways grandma and I were alike, grandma was the head of the family; she was holding things together and now it was my turn. I always thought since I was the older sister I would be able to leave first if something had happened. It did not work out like that after my Sissy left. I became the one who took care of things at home. I blamed grandma for that situation; she robbed me of having a sister. If you really look at the big picture, I was not just robbed of my parents and childhood; I was also robbed of having a sister. I wanted my sister so badly to bear my pain with me.

We could never really bond the way sisters bond because although my sister and I were close, we fought all the time. We never could form a positive relationship because of what our parents did to us. We never even hugged. Having experienced loss does something terrible to the mind. It stays with you like bad smelling fish. I needed Sissy right at that moment and she was not there. I started using more drugs to avoid the emptiness. I wanted to block shit out of my head; I am so good at blocking and avoiding issues. I used marijuana as my escape route. I had to erase my sister out of my mind. At that moment I had no sister, if I did not believe that I could not have been strong. I had to be strong for the kids and my grandmother. I had to be strong for me. How do you erase 17 years away without going crazy? You don't! I used every excuse to stay busy and I did things that gave me instant gratification. I had to constantly feel good so I would not feel bad. Life went on without her; I was focusing on school like never before. I focused on the kids like never before.

I was turning 18 years old and by now I had a routine. I would take care of the kids and go to school. I even considered finding a part-time job. Since grandma did not work nights any longer I was able to look for employment in my senior year of high school. I could not believe I made it to my senior year. It was not easy. I had to go to summer school and night school to get all my credits, but I did it. I was a senior in high school looking for a part-time job. It was hard taking care of the kids and going to school and doing the housework, but I felt I needed a job.

All my friends had one and I hated going home after school. Home was very depressing and all I could think about were the things I had no control over.

I know now why in the black community crime is so high because abuse is very high. We are told to suck it in, we are told to hide those hurt feelings. We are told that telling our family business is against all that we believe. We have to remain strong no matter what. If we fail we are considered betrayers of our families. We release all the abuse through drugs, crime and sports. I had to find a way to release my anxiety so I looked for a job. It was hard for me; I had no experience and no one to guide me. Grandma wanted me to stay home with her and the kids, but I felt I needed to branch out.

I finally landed a part-time job at the Duty Free shop at the JRB airport. This was my first real job and I worked four hours a day after school. It was great; I felt the cord was broken between me and my home. I felt a sense of relief that I was able to do something for me. Grandma was not happy, she raised hell and she stated she needed me at home to help out. Of course, I rebelled and continued to work.

My grades were steady and I was getting close to graduation. I could not believe it. The only thing that was stopping me from graduating was the reading, math and writing RCT. This is a test that you had to pass before getting out of high school. I could not pass these tests for shit. I failed them three times already and had no confidence that I could pass them. I told no one of these test, just as I was scared to take them, I was scared to tell anyone about them. Grandma looked forward to me graduating and making her proud; she did so much for me. I could not let her down. Besides, for once in my life I wanted to make it. I would go home after work and study hard and try to remember what I studied. At that time, to me the test was so hard that I really believed I could not pass. I really believed that I was a loser and I would never amount to anything. The pressure was on me and I felt my back was against the wall.

My so-called family was calling and congratulating me for a diploma I didn't get yet. I had to pass all three of those test before I was able to march at graduation with the rest of the class. My grandmother was the only one who had faith in me. I think she knew something was wrong but she could not pinpoint it, but she believed in me. I see that now, I could not see that then. I thought, she thought I would never make it because she never discussed graduation with me. I believe she did not want to put more pressure on me. My grandmother was the best thing that ever happened to me. I never realized it then, I always knew that I would be loyal to her; but I never knew how much I loved her until this moment.

I slept well the night before the test. I ate a good breakfast, which I never did before and I took the tests at 8am. I was so nervous but I finished all three tests by late afternoon. Graduation was two weeks away. I would get my results the next day when I reached school. The next morning I got to school early. I was so nervous I did not want to check the results, but they were back fast because the test was corrected by computers. When my counselor gave me my results and I saw that I passed all three tests, I thought it was a joke. I thought and still think they gave the test to me. I was never able to pass that test before why and how did I pass it? I kept thinking how did I pass all three tests simultaneously? Anyway, I thought it did not seem real; it had to be God, or the school or both. I still believe I had extra help from somebody that day.

I graduated and my family attended; my grandma, Christian, Brandy; but Little Man could not come because the school was not equipped for wheelchairs. I had a great time. I fucking did it and I definitely got rewarded from my grandmother. After graduation she and I took the kids home and she made dinner for me. I was excited because grandma did not give me my gift that morning and I knew it had to be money because she did not know what I liked. She really fooled me.

During dinner she gave me some tickets and I was scared because I thought grandma was going away and leaving me with the kids. I opened the envelope and read my name on the tickets. I had a round trip ticket to San Juan, Puerto Rico to meet the cruise ship Queen Victoria for an eight day, seven night cruise to six different Islands. I nearly passed the fuck out; grandma went all out for me.

I was 18 and going away for the first time on my own. I was excited as hell; all I could think about was smoking weed on the ship and fucking the captain. I always watched the Love Boat television show and dreamed of being on that fucking ship. The dress attire for the trip was formal. I had to buy evening gowns for every night of the week because you can only come to the dining room formally dressed. After dinner I called all my friends and they were so jealous I could smell it. It was great. Although I was excited about going on the trip, I knew I had nothing planned for when I returned.

Chapter 7

Growing Up

I was working at the Duty Free Shop at JRB airport but I was making only $3.65 an hour and that was part-time. I began to worry about my future. I did remember what the counselor told me about college and I decided to apply for Old Westberk College before leaving on my cruise. Of course, I applied late for college but I thought better late than never. At least applying gave me some comfort, I just did not want to think I would not be doing anything when I returned. It was hard to think about college when I had to think about grandma and the kids.

While preparing for my trip and applying for college I also thought, who will watch the family while I was on my cruise? Who would cook for them and get the kids dressed in the morning. I was hoping maybe my sister would come and help out; I thought maybe I'd call her to get an answer, as soon as possible. I could not sleep the entire night thinking of the trip, my family and my future. I had my best friend with me that night, my joint and I felt warm and cozy inside. After smoking my best friend, I started to glance over the last four years and how my life had changed. I just graduated high school after four years and I completed high school on time. None of my friends completed high school and if they did they had to do four and a half years or five years. This good feeling did not last long because of the other shit I had to worry about that took over my life.

I did not receive a phone call from my father, who by the way, was doing well. He had his own business and became a very successful contractor for a well-known real estate developer, Robert Strack. He always reminded me that his other children came first, he is remarried to a bitch and their kids are set for life. I could not call my mom for help. She was in prison and she was coming home soon, but not in time for me to go on my trip. My sister took no interest in my life, especially when it came to my education. She hated the fact that I never dropped out of school like her. She was the youngest and she was supposed to graduate.

I woke up and I was not sure if I wanted to get up early or lie in bed because school was over and I was not used to it being over. I was about to jump up and get ready for school. That is a scary feeling to wake up and have nowhere to go. It freaked me out; I wondered was life like that. If you don't do anything with your life, your life is nothing. School taught me that the reason we go is to train ourselves to wake up and move on to something every morning. I understood that after graduation. It is important to lead a productive life. I was never taught that. I probably never would have realized that if I hadn't graduated. Graduation gave me an ending to a new beginning. I started something and completed it. That helped me in my journey in life; I was able to move to the next level because I completed high school. It sounds weird but life is really stepping stones.

I finally got the nerve to call my sister and she said she would not come and help grandma with the children while I was on my cruise. She did not even congratulate me for graduating high school; she wished me well and hung up quick. I had all my clothes ready and packed. I took grandma food shopping and bought groceries and snacks for eight days and seven nights. I washed the kid's clothes and cleaned the house so the kids would have fresh clothes for the week. I thought of everything! I even had the church people next door check on my family while I was gone. Grandma was very close to the people at the church. They are the ones who helped organize my cruise. I continued to work at the Duty Free Shop but when I asked them to give me the seven days off for my trip, my boss refused. He told me if I take off seven days, don't come back. I gave this job eight months of my life and that's how I was treated, I told my boss the hell with his job and left the store. They mailed my last check. I was glad because all that time I was stealing cigarettes and when tourists came in the store I gave away free stuff. Even though I was glad to walk away from that job, it left me thinking once again *what would I do when I returned?* I was afraid of not having anything. College was looking more real to me than ever before. I completed all the forms for Old Westberk College and when I returned from my cruise I would have to complete the financial aid forms in order to qualify for room and board.

I had less than ten hours before I left for my cruise. I was ready, able and willing. I bought ten bags of weed, I bought three packs of bamboo paper but I had one dilemma. How the hell was I going to get ten bags of weed on an airplane to San Juan? I figured I would not have to worry about coming back because I would have smoked those ten bags in seven days. I sat up all night thinking how I could smuggle the weed on the plane. I got desperate and begin to panic and then I realized I can put them in a Kotex pad and put it between my legs. First, I put the weed in plastic and put it in inside of a Kotex. It was brilliant! I thought I was so smart when I came up with that idea. I got up early and got dressed, filled the Kotex with weed and put it between my legs and pulled up my panties. I was calling a cab and grandma was calling me. She made me breakfast but I was too excited to eat. I kissed Brandy, Christian and Little Man. I hugged grandma and told her "don't worry, I'll call". I jumped in the cab and said "JRB please". I never said that before and it was great. I got to the airport and was nervous but I walked through the metal detectors and nothing happened. I boarded the plane and I was in like Flynn. My first time on a plane and I'm smuggling drugs. It was so stimulating. I could have sparked a joint or had an organism right there. The flight went fast and I was in San Juan, which was hard as hell because if I had not thought of the Kotex thing I would have been busted. When I arrived to beautiful Puerto Rico, their officers ran i sacked my bags at the airport. They messed up my clothes plus all my shit in my suitcase and to think I was going to put the weed in my suitcase. I was shitting bricks, but of course I got through and was on my way to boarding the Ship, the

Queen Victoria. It was beautiful, four floors of glamour. I went to my room and I thought I had the best room on the ship. I had two beds, a large bathroom and a sitting area all to myself. The first thing I did was put a towel under the door and sparked a fat joint. Then I heard the funniest shit on the loud speaker. I thought I was dreaming. The fucking loud speaker was playing the theme song from the Love Boat television show. It freaked me out and I knew, from that moment on, I was going to have a good time.

I did not unpack before I went down to the bar area and drank like a horse. I was never a drinker, but everything was free so I took advantage. I drank so much I became sick the first night. It wasn't just the alcohol that made me sick it was the ship cruising to the next port. I was seasick; the ship was rocking back and forth so fast. I dragged myself to my room and called room service for seasickness medicine. I was sick in bed all night, but it was still relaxing. No kids, no drama and no noise. The next morning I felt great but I did stay away from the bar. I knew if I wanted to have fun I needed to just stick with the weed and nothing else.

So, for the next couple of days I took morning and afternoon swims, ate top of the line seafood, steak, slept between activities and smoked lots of joints. I was definitely ready to go back home. I had a nice vacation but by the 4th day grandma and the kids were on my mind. I tried calling and could not get through. I tried to relax but I was not used to being away from home. I was definitely homesick. At that time, I thanked God for the weed; it kept me busy. Even though there were a lot of activities on the ship, I either did it all already or was not interested in the activity any longer. I am from the ghetto. What that means to me is that I was not exposed to Marco Polo, Gambling, Swimming and the Country Club bull shit. I could not enjoy that alone without the family.

It was time to return home and during the entire trip I did not speak to grandma and the kids. I knew something was wrong. I was so worried by the last day; I just threw my clothes in the suitcase instead of packing neatly. I was smoking the last bit of weed, making sure I got rid of all that shit. I wanted to go home and nothing was going to stop me. I was glad I did not fold my clothes properly because once again the security at the airport of course ransacked my suitcase. I got to New York and jumped in a yellow cab and when I pulled up in front of the house, my grandma and the kids were waiting outside. I was so relieved, the house was still standing. When I walked in the house I could not believe the mess the kids made. The house was a wreck. They destroyed shit, they broke shit and they left shitty diapers on the floor. My grandma was a very messy person; I can't blame the entire mess on the kids. She never cleaned her room, she never liked to wash dishes and she could live in a dirty house like it was in fashion. The dirt never bothered her and that was scary. It took me hours to clean the house. I was glad I relaxed while on vacation because I had the strength to clean through the night. By the morning I got the bad smell out of the house, clean sheets on the bed, dishes, pots and floors clean. I threw away the broken objects and wrote down what needed to be replaced, such as my stereo, which I had in the living room. They broke it, I was devastated. I cried, I yelled and I cursed. I refused to live in a dirty house. Once I finished cleaning the house I gave them the gifts that I purchased in St. Thomas. Everyone loved their gifts and I loved giving them.

I unlocked my bedroom door and went into my room. My room was clean just the way I left it. Thank God for locks. It was a Sunday when I returned home and I had plans on getting Brandy enrolled in school on Monday as well as completing my financial aid forms for Old Westberk College. The kids and I relaxed. Brandy was five now and Christian was three years old. I was glad Brandy was five, she was out of diapers and she was easier to take care of. She was ready for kindergarten and we were ready to send her. Grandma surprised me with some news, she was in her late 60's and she retired from her job of 35 years. She stated she was bored. She did not want Brandy to start at a big school where she would have to be there from 8 a.m. to 6 p.m. She wanted Brandy to attend school from 8 am to 12 p.m.; but under no circumstances was I going to allow that. Grandma would just have to take up sewing again because no way I wanted Brandy to be home anymore during the day when I was not home. I wanted her bad ass home when I was home so at least the house would stay clean.

I got a ride to Old Westberk College to complete the financial aid forms. The campus was beautiful. I fell in love with the school; it was going to be my home. Aunt Jacky would have to take responsibility for the kids when she came home if I had a chance to go away to college. My mother was getting out soon and maybe she would be able to help out. This was my chance to break away from my family, I thought this was my opportunity to get out and learn how to take care of myself.

The campus had horses, grass and trees everywhere; I did not want to mess this up. I completed the financial aid forms and was informed it would take two weeks before I knew if I was qualified for financial aid. Old Westberk was the only school I picked so if it did not work out, I would not have a future. I wished I had picked other schools but when I was trying to get out of high school, college was the last thing on my mind. I only picked Old Westberk because my mean counselor said I had to pick something. I just blurted out Old Westberk because I heard another student say it was a nice place. I knew nothing about the school. I just knew I had to plan a life for myself after high school.

After completing the forms at Old Westberk I rushed home to tell grandma how beautiful the campus was. She was not interested in me going to college. Especially, if it meant I had to go away to college. She wanted me home with her and the kids. She was not showing any interest, so I discontinued the conversation and started dinner. Grandma was scared for me to leave her. I did not want to think that she did not care about my future. I became angry that I had to be stuck there with her. I thought she would be happy to see me interested in college. But she wasn't, she was more interested in me finding a bullshit job close to home. I rebelled more towards her for her actions that day. But on the other hand I loved her so much I did not truly want to leave her. I wanted to leave the situation. I was the weak one; I believe I was still at home because I fell for all the bullshit.

Although my sister, my mother, Aunt Jacky and their siblings left home, they did not leave on a good note. They left because of drugs, the street life, cops chasing them or thinking they could find something better in a man. It is sad to say that everyone who left this family has not succeeded in life. What makes me think I would make it? Especially, when you don't have a positive role model in your life and it becomes one hundred times easier to believe that you will fail. That was my biggest problem, I had faith in nothing; I had nothing to believe in. The only time I called on God back then was when I was in trouble. All the strength that I had to succeed came from within, I wanted a better life at the time and I knew it when I did not allow myself to live in a dirty house. I wanted a better, cleaner, richer life. I only had the strength when I needed it; I needed it or called upon it only when I wanted something. It wasn't like I lived my life with strength on a daily basis; in that case I would have been drug free.

It was hard for me because I felt sorry for myself for many years. Every time I felt myself falling I would jump up like there was a fire under my ass. My motivation wasn't or isn't pure motivation, I'm a chicken when it comes to reality. I knew one day grandma would not be able to take care of me and that scared the shit out of me. I knew if I did not get it together, it would be harder for me trying to make it after she was gone. So, I thought I better take care of me now before it was too late, like the old saying, "it's always better to look for a job while you have a job," less pressure.

I took Brandy to the dentist, she had great teeth already. She was only five years old but her teeth grew in perfectly. The dentist stated she just needed a cleaning and sent us on our way. Brandy received all her shots and I registered her into kindergarten. Brandy did not want to go to school, she was very defiant and she was very angry all the time. Brandy grew fond of my grandmother and she loved grandma to death. When she found out she was going to be enrolled into school she cried for days. She did not want to leave the house. I believed at the time she thought no one would come and pick her up. She kept asking me, if I was going to leave her at school. I used to scare her and say, "Yes", if she doesn't stop breaking my stuff. Brandy suffered from her mother leaving her. She needed her mother, I was too young and grandma was too old. We could never discipline her, hell I needed someone to discipline me. I was doing shit I was not supposed to be doing but there was no one there to say, "Don't do that". Grandma babied me and the kids, anything we wanted that she was able to afford, we got it. When the kids messed up the house or broke my shit, she would replace it or say, "They're kids; they are supposed to make a mess". I used to get mad because she NEVER disciplined them. She never yelled at the kids. It was always hugs and kisses with grandma. Hugs and kisses are great, but every kid needs discipline.

Christian was just coming out of diapers; he was very quiet and he was nothing like Brandy. He was passive, he needed attention and he got it through being quiet and cute. Christian did not talk as much as Brandy did. He was withdrawn; he was not as active as his sister. And at that time, it made me happy. I did not need him to be active like his sister. Then there was Little Man who was very quiet; he could not walk or talk so he just sat in the bed. He was depressing; he made me cry a lot. I stayed sad when I was around him. With him it was a special kind of love, he was my baby brother. I felt helpless and hopeless when it came to him. He just sat there asking for nothing. It was like looking at an angel. He was so beautiful, I never saw such a handsome little boy.

I finally heard from Old Westberk College, they informed me that I was accepted into their college and that I was approved for full financial aid. As I read the letter, I started crying. I could not believe I was going away to college. I had nothing ready, I had to buy clothes for the winter and I needed college stuff. My orientation was in one week and I never really told grandma how serious I was about attending college. I prepared myself for orientation the following week. I was nervous and I smoked a pack of cigarettes and smoked a joint before leaving. I was a bit sad because I knew I was not college material, nor did I have money to buy the things I needed for college... but I went.

Addiction "Aunt Jacky"

I got to the school and we went on a tour of the campus before the important shit was discussed such as classes and tuition. After brunch, we were all escorted to the lounge to discuss the tuition. I was excited that everything was going well. Then my name was called by an advisor. She had a file on me which included my application forms, my high school diploma and my financial aid forms. She looked over everything and stated everything looked good. But when it came time for me to discuss room and board I did not qualify. She explained that the financial aid forms were not in on time and my room was not paid for so I would either have to pay for the room up front or I would have to travel back and forth to school every day. There was no way I could do either. Room and board was too much for me to think of paying for and how could I travel back and forth to school when the ride is three to four hours each way. I could not even ask grandma for the money because she was on a fixed income. My father was a good resource; I decided to try calling him when I returned home. I took the Bluehound bus back to New York, which gave me three hours to think about my life. I did not want to call my father, but he was my last resort. I did not think this plan through. I did not even tell grandma I was planning on leaving for college. I thought, what would she do without me? I cried so much on that bus. I started to light a joint when I realized I was on the bus. I carried weed with me wherever I went, it was my best friend.

I called my father as soon as I got home; it turned out to be a bad idea. He had no interest in financially supporting my college education. His excuse was that he was saving money for his other kids to attend college. He actually said that I should not put him on any of my applications because the school will know he has his own business and that they will try and make him pay. I was in shock, this man never seemed to amaze me, to top it off he came over that evening and did something to me that was unimaginable. He knew I was distraught; he came and gave me a couple of hundred dollars for my high school graduation. He didn't realize I graduated from high school until that day. I guess he felt guilty and did what he normally did when he felt guilty, he gave me money. Not enough to make it but enough for me to get high. At least, that is what I used the money for.

When he came to my house that night to bring the money, he had other intentions that blew my fucking mind. I refused to see him when he first arrived. The kids never really knew my father so when he rang the bell they made him wait at the door. Grandma convinced me to let him in. After unlocking my bedroom door, I laid across the bed. My father said "hello" to grandma. I heard them talking and I closed my bedroom door. He then knocked on my door and said, "Congratulations!" I did not respond. He sat on the edge of my bed and started telling me how bad his business was doing. I knew he was lying. He had a brand new truck and he looked well off. He gave me a couple of hundred dollars and asked me for a hug. I gave it to him and I tried to pull away quickly, but he held on tight. I thought he missed me until his hands started to move down my back, it did not feel like a fatherly hug. Not that I had plenty of fatherly hugs but I did know a bad feeling when I felt one. This hug did not feel right. I pushed away and he got up and left. I thought about that hug all night but I dismissed it by the morning because I had bigger fish to fry. By the time the morning kicked in, I was depressed. School was starting in two weeks and I had nowhere to go. I bought some weed early that morning and smoked weed in bed the entire day. I was becoming lazy as hell; I thought I had nothing to live for.

Chapter 8

Independence

I was glad that Brandy would be able to start school. She wasn't happy; but I was. I had to figure out what was I going to do. I figured I would look for a job in the meantime. Old Westberk did not turn me down; they just said I was not qualified for financial aid for my room and board for the first semester. I could always attend school during the spring semester.

I went to the mall and completed job applications to work at Alexander's' department store. There were jobs available because all the college kids returned to school. I was hired to work at Alexander's for $4.15 an hour. Grandma was happy with me working at Alexander's because I was close to home and earning my own money. I was supposed to start the job in a couple of days, but I was not happy about working there. I felt at the time I had no choice. I actually cried when they hired me. I cried because I wanted more than Alexander's, I wanted a career. I thought I would be stuck there working behind a counter for the rest of my life.

It was Brandy's first day of school and I took her to her new school. She was very nervous and she cried the whole way there. She asked me to stay with her for part of the day; I told her I would. It was a Kodak moment, something Aunt Jacky never got to see. She did not get to witness her daughter's first day of school. Brandy looked so cute with her jumpsuit and matching hat. I bought her a designer book bag and she loved it so much. Brandy's school was big for a kindergarten class and I would have been scared too if I was her. There were such big kids in the class. Brandy was very small for her age and I did not want to leave her. She cried and I cried. The teacher told me I would have to leave because it made things worse. I cursed that bitch out. I was worried about my Brandy and she's telling me to leave. I left because I did not want to cause any trouble, but I told that teacher I would be back to pick up Brandy. I told Brandy, "don't worry I'll be back". I cried on my way home and I could not believe that I was crying. That moment right there showed me how much I loved that little girl. I could not ever imagine leaving my child as my mother did me and the way Aunt Jacky left Brandy. I decided to walk home instead of taking the bus. It was nice out and I had nothing else planned for the day.

As I was walking, I ran into Michelle. Our friendship had not been as strong as it was when we first met in high school, but I was sure glad to see her. She graduated a year earlier than I did and with me working after school and taking so many classes to graduate on time, I stopped calling as much as I used to. But we still loved each other and we both were glad to see one another. She informed me about what she was doing with her life since graduation. She stated that she applied to Heights University and she got in; I was impressed with HU. Michelle stated she was very happy there and they have good counselors who can help you. She asked me about Old Westberk because she knew I had applied but I never told her the outcome. I explained to her what had happen and she stated that at HU you would not need room and board money because I could stay home rather than living on campus. Michelle stated that since I have my financial aid approved for tuition that was all I would need. Since I had time that morning, Michelle took me over to HU right that second. She was on her way to school and she invited me for a tour.

It was not Old Westberk but it was great. I did like the atmosphere; I thought it was very calming. Michelle went to meet with her advisor but before she went she took me to the admissions office. I completed an application, gave them $25.00 and wrote an essay on why I wanted to attend college. I was than escorted to the financial aid office by the admission's counselor and they checked the computer and saw that I was qualified to receive full tuition. I was then sent back to the admissions office and they explained to me that I would have to bring my transcript and diploma to them ASAP to be considered for their undergraduate program. The woman stated, once I did that they would determine if I could be accepted into the college. Once I heard that, I became quickly discouraged because I figured they would not accept me because the first two years of high school I did not do well. I went home and thought about it and thought *what the hell, just try.*

I had an hour before Brandy had to be picked up so I started to clean the house and make dinner. Grandma was on the porch waiting for Little Man to come home. She asked me what took me so long to get home this morning; I did not tell her that I went to HU so I just said that I ran into Michelle and we had breakfast. Grandma loved Michelle; she knew Michelle did not use drugs and was basically good. I did not want to say anything about HU because I was not sure I was getting in. If I did get in, grandma would love it. I would be able to stay home and help out, along with going to college.

Grandma was waiting patiently for Little Man and I decided to let grandma watch the food while I picked Brandy up from school. Brandy was miserable, she hated school that day. She must have cried the entire day. She said her teacher yelled at her and she's not going back. I tried to talk to Brandy and convince her that school can be fun and she can learn a lot of things. She did not want to hear it.

Something was strange when we got home; grandma was still waiting for my Little Man. She called the school and no one answered. My brother was 12 years old but since he could not walk or talk we both begin to panic. It just did not feel right; He was an hour and a half late. We finally received a phone call from the director of the school. They told my grandmother there was an accident and she has to meet them at the hospital. Grandma left me with the kids and took a cab to the hospital. I thought it would not have been as serious as it was because they did not tell her anything over the phone.

Independence

My grandmother left for the hospital and never called me to tell me what happened. I waited for her for hours before she got home. When she returned dinner was over, the kids were asleep and I had waited on the couch for the news. When she walked in the house her face told the story of a woman in pain. I asked what happened; she didn't have Little Man with her. She said he was gone, that was all I got out of her. She burst into tears and this was the first time I saw grandma hopeless. I did not know what to do, I called my sister in San Francisco and told her what had happened, but I did not know what really happened so I could not give her any details. My sister then talked to grandma and grandma told her that Little Man died at school. My grandmother began to scream; she was screaming to God and asking why, why did he take Little Man. Once she calmed down she started to call friends and other family members. I could not believe it; I was so hurt, I cried for hours. After speaking to the pastor, she was able to tell me the story.

While at school my baby brother choked on his lunch and no one knew he was choking and could not save him in time. Actually, they found him dead when it was time to prepare the children to go home. This is why it took so long for us to find out. This news was the saddest news my family ever heard. My grandmother never imagined him going before her. She thought he was going to be around for a long time. Especially since he lived passed the time the doctors gave her for him to live. I made all the funeral arrangements with my grandmother; I bought the suit he would wear. I bought him an all white suit with a white shirt and a white tie. The reason for the white was because he was our angel, he was innocent and he was a virgin to life. Although my mother was getting out of prison in a few weeks, the officials at Wedford Hills allowed her to attend her son's funeral. These were the darkest days for us. Losing an innocent child due to negligence is one of the worst feelings. My grandmother was never the same. She gave a lot to my brother and she was losing the ones she loved too fast. Everything she worked for and believed in was disappearing before her eyes. I felt very close to grandma at this time and was glad I did not go away to college.

Addiction "Aunt Jacky"

I was trying to cope with the death of my brother when my sister decided to stay with the family after the funeral. She was getting along well with grandma and I was very glad. They did not argue at all in the beginning. My sister looked well; she was getting older and had a steady job. She was in love with the China man and they had their own home in San Francisco. She showed us pictures and her place looked very nice. She was 18 going on 19 years old, but the way she carried herself, I thought I was talking with an older woman. She surprised the family and told everyone she was getting married and that she was two months pregnant. I was glad I was able to see her and spend time with her. She could not stay long but I enjoyed her visit. Grandma on the other had resented the fact that she left. She never forgave my sister and I could hear the sarcasm in grandma's voice when she talked to my sister.

My grandmother felt betrayed and I believed she was hurt. It was not easy caring for her children's children and for my sister to be ungrateful was very disappointing to her. I thought the news of my sister being pregnant would soften my grandma's heart, but it just seemed to make her more angry and bitter. My sister on the other hand did not care about that; she was not like me. She would not or could not tolerate the bullshit, and when she saw her chance to leave, she took it. She was not able to cope; she would have had a nervous breakdown if she would have stayed home. She was getting in too deep with grandma and by dropping out of high school, her self esteem was shot. My sister's education was her pride and joy at one time. She always had great grades; she always was at the top of her class. I was the one who always struggled with my class work. My sister was brilliant. She was someone who never had to study to pull straight A's.

I finally received my letter from HU. I was afraid to open it, so I went to my room and lit a joint and then opened it. They accepted me as a non-matriculated student; they wanted to see how I would do the first semester and if I did well they would consider accepting me as a matriculated student in the spring. In other words, they were testing me to see if I could hack it and if I could they would take a chance on me. Once again, I was given an opportunity I could not afford to take advantage of, no matter what. I could not believe I was going to HU.

I started classes two weeks late but I was eager to begin. Even though grandma was sad about Little Man's death, she was proud; she bragged to everyone that I was in college. I never heard her boast about one of her children. I had all her attention and she focused on me. HU was great and I met new friends. I was able to hang with Michelle again and I had flexible classes. I did not have a major, but I knew I wanted to make it. I was doing well; I never let myself slack up. I wanted to focus on having good grades so I would not be in jeopardy of being dismissed from college.

I gathered a group of students to form a study group. These are the friends I only hung out with at school. We studied together and we helped each other with our assignments. I knew right away I was going to need help. I wasn't exactly college material. I wasn't ashamed of that since I used drugs most of my educational life and the other part was I was not interested in learning; I believed I was only interested in the outcome and I didn't mind because the outcome was great. I enjoyed studying with the group, I felt smart. We would go over ideas and learn things I never imagined. This was the side of me that I enjoyed. Having a clean atmosphere is very positive and I never met so many drug-free people. The entire group did not do drugs. I, of course acted as if I never heard of the shit. I felt I did not need people to judge me because of my addiction. I no longer wanted to burden people with my problems. I dealt with them on my own. If I wanted to smoke a joint, I would wait until I was home. Life was better this way, people began to notice me and it gave me more confidence to showcase my intelligence.

Even with the kids, I helped my grandma as much as I could. By now my mother was home but she was up to her old tricks a week into her release. The only thing I did get from her was precious gifts. She always sent me money or beautiful pocketbooks and clothes. She was proud of me for attending a four year college. Not just any college but HU, I guess she thought I would have never gotten that far. No one actually expected me to get that far, all the odds were against me.

Brandy was having difficulty in school; I was at her school on a regular basis. Her attitude was so rude and the school officials were trying to decide if they were going to place her into a Special Education class. They stated that she was too angry to learn. She needed counseling so she would be able to sit still and learn. I was 19 years old and I didn't have a clue what Special Education meant. The way they described it, Brandy would be in a classroom with specialized teachers and a few other kids in the class room. It was supposed to help her but all it did was knock her self-esteem to the ground. I was angry because I knew why Brandy was angry, she wanted her mother. She hated that the other kids would tease her about her mother not living with her. She felt she had to do bad things or act out to get attention. She constantly needed attention. Brandy needed her parents, not me and grandma. On the other hand, Christian was doing well; he was a good kid. He was very quiet and was just into messing up the house, he was never as destructive as Brandy but he kept me busy. Between the kid's medical appointments and caring for the house, I felt like a regular housewife without the husband.

I wasn't dating, I had not had a date in years; I lost weight and had a brand new look. I was not as interested in men as I used to be. I did not mind that I was not dating, I enjoyed loving me. I masturbated every night for two years and that was comforting for me. I think I fell in love with me; I would have intimate nights with myself. Wine, cheese, weed and music were enough. I was focused on other things and since the Ryan thing I never really thought about sex. When I was with Ryan he never focused on sex, I think I can count the times we had sex. With him it was touching and talking. That's what made me fall for him so quickly. Every man before him focused on sex. Before Ryan, sex was disgusting to me and I thought I would never enjoy it again. Ryan made it pleasurable; he did not want it all the time. Even when we slept together at my house on most occasions, we just cuddled. I can truly say my relationship with Ryan was great. I learned how a woman should be treated in regards to sex. I never felt pushed or smothered sexually and with my background that was very important in my first real sexual relationship. He actually did set the tone for all my boyfriends thereafter.

As time passed, I was becoming less attracted to men. I would meet guys all the time on campus but they were either jocks which I hated, rich kids who were only interested in themselves and nerds. I felt my sexuality changing; I felt a difference in me. I did not pay attention to it; this feeling came upon me many times before but I ignored it. I did notice that I was not yearning for a man but I was aroused when I saw a beautiful woman. I did not know why at the time but I was. I was too ashamed to think of that so I refused to think about sex in general.

One day I came home from school and grandma informed me that she was going back to work. She stated she could not sit home and just wait to die. She informed me that she called a few home attendant agencies and was interviewed for a job. She stated she was waiting for them to call her back. This woman was pushing 70 years old. Who would hire her? She was too old to take care of old people. She should have had someone taking care of her. She has not been the same since Little Man died and she explained that she was bored. She worked two jobs for thirty eight years. How could she just sit home watching television? I knew we did not need the money; grandma got three different checks a month plus money for the kids. She had a large insurance policy that she cashed in after my brother died. She had a check to pay the bills, one for rent and one for shopping expenses. I took care of myself and gave her money every month for my bedroom. I applied for welfare since I was enrolled into college and received $176.00 every two weeks in cash and $100.00 in food stamps which I gave to grandma every month. Grandma was very happy about the food stamps since it was just me, her and the kids; that $100.00 went very far. She allowed me to keep the $176.00 in cash for my college expenses, carfare, beeper, home phone and clothes. So I knew grandma did not need the money, she wanted to work because she wanted to; she was addicted to doing something. I was glad she was energetic at her age but I wished she would have put all that energy in helping raise the kids and keeping our home clean. Instead she preferred to clean other people's homes and complained when she got home that our home was not clean enough. I never understood that. I got used to grandma not working, I hated when she worked when I was a child. It left me vulnerable in the house alone. I was unhappy that she picked night work because this meant she would have to stay with the patient through the night. She loved that she got the night shift. She was home during the day to watch her soap operas and at night she had her job. She would talk about her patients all day if you let her. Grandma just had to work, that was all she knew, she could never just sit still even though she needed to and deserved to.

I had to help Brandy with her homework when I got home. I was attending college full time and working part-time. I was very busy; I could only hang out at night when grandma had her two days off. She tried to work the days she had off but I threatened to leave and she forgot about that idea. School was great; Michelle was becoming discouraged because she was not doing well so she joined my study group. She continued to live at home with her parents. Michelle's parents' drug problems' were getting worse; and their problems were getting to her. The worst thing with Michelle's parents was that they would get high, go home and nod all day and that would piss Michelle off. I know for sure I could not sit in a room with my mother while she was high off heroin. It made me sick just to talk with her, I hated it. Michelle had to live with it and it drove her crazy. She would come to the study group and cry or she would just leave.

She was not doing well on her exams and was facing academic probation. We talked and I convinced her not to drop out. She went and talked with our school counselor. He advised her to take some summer courses and she could bring up her average. I offered to take some summer courses with her so she would not be by herself. The group also offered to take summer courses so we all would be together. The group was very supportive; we all wanted each other to graduate and they always pitched in to help.

Michelle's school problem was fixed but she knew she still had to face her parents after school. She wanted to move out of their house, but all she had was a minimum wage job and that was part-time. She could not afford to move out with having only a part-time job. She wanted to quit school and work full time. She decided to put the move on hold and see how the college thing worked out. I told her if she graduates from college she would have a better chance of leaving her parents' house than if she left college early. Although I was fulfilled by the group, I was missing my old life style. I was in love with my new life but my old ways kept pulling me towards the life I ran from.

Chapter 9

Hanging Tuff

One day I decided to look up some of my old friends from high school; most of them went to work after leaving high school. They had no plans for college and half of them were drop-outs. The other half became law enforcement officers. They were my street friends. Even though my street friends did not have college degrees they had jobs. Kim was a senior when I was a freshman in high school. She and her friends, after graduating high school, took the city and state exams to become probation and correction officers. It did not matter to me what they did because I was a college student. Even though Kim did not hang out with my crew at Thomas Harding High School, she knew of me and I knew of her.

I would study during the week and hang out on the weekends. I would help at home with the kids, get them ready for school, prepare dinner and clean the house. This was my routine for years. The only time it became a problem was when my mother would come and bring her friends over to stay, or when Brandy was acting out in school and I'd have to run to her school and fix whatever problem she caused. Other than that my college life was sweet. Once I became comfortable studying with my group I was able to party more. I hooked up with my old friends from high school and I started to enjoy hanging out again; they had badges, cars and money. They were three and four years older than I, but we were still close in age.

At that time, the police department was hiring right out of high school. Instead of my street friends going to college as I did, they chose to work and earn money. Nothing wrong with that; but the things we were into interfered more with their careers than mine. They had to hide what they did because they held positions of authority. There were five of us. Kim Brown, who held a job at Wikers Island as a correction officer for about five years, was a couple of years older than me and she had three kids. I never really had a friend who had kids up until I met Kim. Kim was an okay mom; she had a good job and she genuinely loved her kids. But Kim had a big drug habit that, in some ways, affected how she raised her children. Kim was a senior at my high school when I was a freshman. Back then we barley talked, but she somehow knew my background from the streets and trusted me to come into her crew. Kim was engaged to be married and she was very much in love with her fiancée who knew nothing of her drug problem.

Stanley was Kim's fiancée. He was a law school student who was at the top of his class. He loved Kim and their three children. Stanley was the father of all Kim's children and that was something they both were proud of. Stanley was a committed law student and he came from a family of lawyers. Stanley's father was a lawyer, his grandfather was a lawyer and now Stanley was about to be a lawyer. Kim was from the hood and she never saw Stanley's worth as I did. Kim was just glad to have a city job that paid the bills because, at the time, Stanley was living off his parents and Kim. She did not see that once he completed law school they were going to be the next Cosbys. I envied their relationship; I knew they were going to make it big together as a team. Stanley loved Kim because she was part of the law enforcement team and they could talk for hours about the law. Stanley was in the dark about Kim's drug problem and Kim hid her problem as best she could. Kim had her own apartment and Stanley stayed home with his parents, but most days and nights he was at Kim's apartment either with the kids or with Kim.

Then there was David Brenner, we called him Dee. He held a job as a correction officer at Wedford Hills Correctional Facility in upstate New York for one year before being transferred to Sandville correctional facility. He was young, but he was two years older than I was. Dee's parents hated his job; they wanted Dee to be a doctor in America. They wanted their son to have status in America. Dee dropped out of college his second year and became an officer. Dee did not need the correction officer's job; his parents had plenty of money. They were from Africa and had a small diamond mine.

Dee's parents were very upset that he chose to be a correction officer. He was born in Africa and his parents traveled back and forth from Africa. Dee decided to attend school in America and stayed in his family's house. Dee was used to having money and cars; but once he became serious about being a correction officer, his parents cut his allowance. They thought that would change his mind about his job. But they did not realize that Dee did not become a correction officer for the glamour or the money like most people in the hood, he became a correction officer because he was gay. Dee had to hide this from his parents; Dee would have died if his parents knew he was gay. He would have had nothing.

At least they were paying for the house he lived in and they did not cut him out of their will. Dee would inherit loads of money when his parents died. He did not care about money because he did not have to. Dee knew that it would have been all over if his parents knew he was fucking inmates on the night shift at Sandville. Dee loved his job. I never saw anyone loving their job as much as Dee did. Dee even slept with some of the married male correction officers on the downlow. He would tell us everything, all about his rendezvous' in the dark with his numerous lovers. It shocked me; I was amazed at how he wore two different hats. He was actually no different from me; my life at school, my life at home and my life with my friends were all different.

Dee and I connected one night; this brought us a little closer. Dee knew my mother since he was placed in upstate New York at Wedford Hills for one year. My mother was placed in Wedford Hills for many years for her crimes and for one of those years Dee briefly came into contact with her. I could not believe it. One night we were getting high and we got into a little family history. I told him my mother's name and how she was once locked up at Wedford Hills and Dee's face froze. He said, "Oh shit! I know your mom; she got mad respect when she was in Wedford Hills." Dee said, "I knew you looked familiar".

Then there was Karen Epstein, she was the probation officer who grew up in the hood and was considered PWT, "poor white trash". She hated her job. She was a probation officer for five years and for three of those years she was out on maternity leave twice and medical injury leave twice. Both times she was on medical leave because she fell on the job which consisted of three and a half years out of work with pay. Probation was looking for an excuse to fire Karen but she always won her case. When she did work, she did go on time and she never missed a day once she was on a groove. Besides, she was Jewish and it seemed like Karen got away with things other officers couldn't. Karen hated her job and she found every excuse not to go to work; but she knew it paid well and without a college education she knew she would be somewhere flipping burgers.

Karen was legally married; she wasn't shacking up with her baby's daddy. Her husband was a State Trooper and he loved his job but he could not support Karen and the two kids alone on his salary. Karen had a drug problem and her husband, Mathew knew nothing. She pretended to be the soccer mom but on the side she was doing as much cocaine as we were. Karen was different though, her family was poor. Her mother died when she and her brother were young. Her father owned a shoe repair shop that barely paid the bills. Karen used to say she was playing housewife way before she got married. Karen's father never remarried and Karen had to fulfill the duties her mother left behind. As Karen would have explained it, she was a mother to her baby brother and a wife to her father. Karen was looking for a way out after high school; she stated if she did not get out she would have gotten pregnant by her father because he did not use protection when he had sex with her.

Karen got out; she got married and lived in a good neighborhood. Both she and her husband were white and Jewish so they were able to get into a better neighborhood, even though they were making the same money the other officers made. She had a large four-bedroom house, her kids played soccer on the weekends and Karen was the team mom. She would pick up all the kids in her minivan, buy juices and water for every game and wash the team uniforms weekly.

Last but not least, there was Harper Mitchell, she was beautiful. She was light skinned, with an hourglass figure. She had no children and she was raised by her grandmother who she cared for when she became an adult. Harper was kind, young and energetic and she loved being a police officer. She got us into clubs, out of traffic tickets and we got mad respect from the Columbians whom we were buying cocaine from in Spanish Harlem. Harper loved her lifestyle. She slept around and I think the cocaine helped justify her sleeping around. She had no boundaries. The only person that cared for her was her grandmother who was getting older by the minute. Harper was looking for love and I think her having sex with different men made her feel the love she never got from her parents. Harper was raised in foster care for a couple of years until her grandmother found her. Harper's mother was a crack-head who had an apartment in the projects and she lived off welfare. She never told Harper's grandmother where Harper was. It took Harper's grandmother two years to get Harper out of foster care. Harper's dad was nowhere to be found. Rumor has it that he was killed for stealing and running off with some drug dealer's drugs when he was supposed to be delivering them. His body was never found and I think that is why Harper wanted to be a cop to find her father.

Harper knew her mother and she would give her mother money here and there to keep her away from her precinct. Harper was gun crazy; she was the gun carrying type. I had to beg her to keep her gun home but when we rode in the car, nobody said anything. Harper liked being a police officer but I could not understand why she did drugs. I'm not talking about weed; we did cocaine for two years straight.

Karen, Harper, Dave and Kim had a lot to lose so they had to put a lot of trust in one another to assure that their secret would be safe. They only trusted me to come into the group because Kim vouched for me. They never trusted me, but they liked me and that was enough for me. Not only were they putting their lives in jeopardy but they were at risk of losing their jobs.

It was ironic; they picked up the drug habit from their jobs. They got free cocaine from the other officers. It happened first at the officer's parties. It was better for them to use cocaine because it only took two days to clean their system. They were all pot-heads until they became officers. I was the only one who kept smoking weed. At first I was scared of the cocaine. I never put anything in my nose. For a long time I would just take freezes, I would put the cocaine on my wrist and lick it and my tongue would be numb. That is what we called taking a "freeze", or I would smoke a cigarette with cocaine in it. Eventually, I was just like them. I started to snort it like everyone else.

School was going great. The first semester was ending and I pulled all B's. Shit I was so happy; I thought I wouldn't get that far. I fucking passed all my classes in college but my study group was smarter. They pulled B+ and A's but I did not give a fuck. I wanted to get the fuck out of college with a degree not just a drug habit. I suffered a lot in my writing class; I could never focus on my writing. I got a C- and I had to take it over because I did not pass the English proficiency test. It was okay though; I went to college thinking I should be grateful to have the opportunity. That English test did not bother me, even though I had to take it four times before passing it.

College life was great. I could not express how I felt at home about college. I could only express myself when I was with my study group. I valued the study group because they were so clean and pure; I looked up to them because of their sheltered lives. Right off the bat, I could tell that their parents cared for them at birth. They were nurtured and loved, and were able to function independently without too many crutches.

Look at Virginia Blackwell. She was one of the study group members and she was as beautiful as her name. She was smart. She wanted to become a businesswoman and own her own business. Her face was dark and flawless. She had a figure eight body that every man wanted but could not have because she was a virgin. I used to tease her and call her Virgi. She was five feet seven and had a sexy ass walk but she did not know she walked sexy. She had an addiction but it was not drugs, it was shopping. That girl spent so much of her parents' money in college with her no working lazy ass.

She drove her parents back to the south and they left her their house in the City. She had to have everything. She loved buying new clothes, pocketbooks, anything name-brand she had to have. I loved Virgi. We were Libras and we connected right away. I liked her because no matter how hard she tried she was a nerd and she hated being one. I did not try to encourage her not to be a nerd because I knew what the other life was like and I had no intentions of introducing her to it. She wanted to try marijuana one day, which is what she called it. I scared her on what it does to you if she smoked it. I told her not to trust anyone with marijuana because they could poison her. Ever since then she never asked me for drugs again. That was the way I liked her, drug free.

Then there was Kevin Sanchez, a pretty boy who I was in love with and knew I would never be able to fuck. The first day we met was in Art class. He could not find his art pencils and I quickly gave him mine. He gravitated to me like a chum, one of the guys. I quickly knew that when he said, "hi". He was confident and he was tough. If this boy liked me, he hid it very well. I knew this would be a friend and I kept it like that.

He was another one who had upper middle class parents. He was from Argentina; his father was a dentist and his mother was a homemaker. Kevin was very spoiled. He had a nice car, he went to private schools his entire academic life and he dressed so preppy. You thought he discovered GQ preppy himself. His skin had pimples because he had a skin problem but he had a nice complexion, jet black curly hair and was good to look at. His addiction was women. He wanted to fuck every beautiful woman he saw or that saw him. All the girls at college loved him but he wanted Virgi and I hated that.

Last but not least was Benny Faulkner. He was the one who had to wear shoes that matched his sweater. His mother raised him and they were very close. I believe that Ben was very comfortable around his mother because she accepted him for whom he was. Ben was smart, he pulled good grades and he wanted to be a geologist.

Ben's addiction was being popular. He was heavy into fashion and that's how he became popular. Ben was gay and no one at school figured it out. He lied about being gay the entire four years of college. He would go to gay clubs and be seen by other students at school but he denied it. I did not mind, nor did the other group members. We never brought it up because we played a dirty trick on him one night to see if the rumors were true and we felt horrible afterwards. Since then we had enough respect for his privacy to never mention that night.

One night we called Ben and pretended to be a guy he met in a club and he went along with it. He really was talking to Kevin but he did not know it. Ben poured out his feelings to Kevin thinking Kevin was a man he met in a night club. Ben said things we never heard a man tell another man before. It dawned on us that Ben liked being fucked up his ass and we had to accept it. We did and moved on and vowed to never talk to Ben about that evil trick we pulled.

We were a great team. We worked together and everyone had fun while studying. We had our own booth in the library that I made sure I reserved. Even the fucking Librarians did not let anyone sit at our booth. We were regulars. We would study three to four hours a day, three days a week.

Chapter 10

Old Enough to Know

Roni called, I hadn't spoken to her in months. I was surprised to hear from her. She said that she had gotten a promotion on her job and was making more money. Roni told me that she had to pay rent since her mother had gotten worse. Her mother's crack problem became Roni's problem. Roni had to pay all the bills in the house because her mother's income vanished as soon as she got her welfare check. She would smoke it up in crack.

Her mother's income also was not steady because she would miss her welfare appointments and they would cut her off every other month. Roni was glad to have the responsibility; she said she now had more say so about who may come in and out of the house. Prior to Roni taking over the bills her mother had folks in the house smoking crack while Roni was at work. Since Roni's mother had refused to go into a treatment program, her mother now had to leave the house when Roni went to work.

Roni sounded good. It appeared she was happy, even though she had drama in her life. She sounded as if all this drama had matured her. Although Roni had to be tough with her mother, she loved her mother and was worried about her mother. Roni's mother always drank Gin, she never used to smoke crack to Roni's knowledge. I think this bothered Roni more than she let on. I did not focus on that. Roni needed to deal with that on her own in Roni's own way. Having a mother on drugs is very difficult and you, as the child, have to learn to deal with it as best as you can. I don't ever remember feeling sorry for

Roni; she did what she had to do. She did not fall under the pressure of having to take over her home and having to make adult decisions at an early age. Roni was a survivor and she did well at work because she had to.

However, she did inform me that she had met a sugar daddy, he had loads of money and she was spending it. She was actually considering buying a car, I was so jealous. Not only did she land somebody who took care of her financially, she loved him. She wanted me to meet him and I told her I would be in Staten Island very soon to meet this new man in her life. Roni then asked about me and I told her about my new moves.

I told her about the college thing, which she was not interested in hearing about. I was surprised to hear her reaction, it sounded as if she was bored when I talked about me going to college. I quickly skipped that subject and went on to my officer friends that I wanted her to meet. She loved that idea; she liked the fact that they had jobs and could get cocaine easily. I did not know Roni knew what cocaine was at the time. She said everyone uptown was doing it. She did it a couple of times at parties. It was definitely a party drug in those days. Everyone who did it went to clubs, dressed up and passed the bill filled with cocaine.

It was all new to the both of us, but we liked it. It was associated, at the time with big Willie's, the big shots who hung out in clubs. Everyone I knew wanted to be in the clubs. I don't know how we started associating the cocaine with clubbing. I only know we mostly used it at the clubs in the beginning. We were getting high before going to the club and while we were at the club. This gave us a feeling of power over men. We would pull all the fly guys, they would take us to breakfast and we would ditch them. Roni and I decided to meet up before the Christmas holiday was over.

School was just about to end for the holidays. Everyone was giving their Christmas gifts and I was sad to leave my study group. They helped me keep everything in perspective. They were my school friends and at times I needed them. I needed to be around them, they made me feel safe. I knew once school ended I would not see them until next semester. They made plans to either go away or be with their families as they did every year. Kevin was going home to Argentina with his family. As he would say, "he is going home". I never really understood that because I always thought he was home. I learned that if you're not from this country, the place you were born in is your home.

Virgi was going skiing with her parents, she had it made, who knew black people skied. Ben was spending the holidays with his mom in Vegas, only Ben and his mother could do Vegas together, I mean Ben was gay and they were the perfect couple. Ben's mother loved him and accepted him and that was unusual. I was embarrassed to tell the group that I never went away for the holidays and that my family could not afford to do holiday trips. We did not have a timeshare anywhere like the college kids. My family, for the holidays, for fun would sit around the house eating fattening foods and opening gifts. When my study group asked me what were my family and I doing for the holidays, I made up another lie and said this year my family was coming to my house because we never get to see them. I told them it would be like a family reunion and that all my family was flying to New York that year.

The only thing I hated about the study group was that we had only one thing in common, our interest in learning and getting our college degree. Other than that we had nothing in common, we came from different backgrounds. These people had successful parents who traveled and exposed their children to a life I could never imagine. I was okay with that because I just wanted to learn from them. They taught me how normal sober people lived and I loved it. They made me feel normal.

I could not wait to get home to start my holiday. I knew what my grades were, so I did not have to wait for the mail like the other students; I had talked to all my professors before school ended that week. My mother decided to drag her sorry ass home for the holidays; she always managed to come home for Christmas when she was not locked up. This shit was okay when I was a kid but I was not happy to see her. When she did come home, she always brought gifts as if that erases the fucked up shit she did all her life as a parent. That year she must have felt guilty, she brought me a silver fox coat, expensive hand bag sets and a pair of suede pants for Christmas. She was guilty because I made it to college and she did not help me get there.

When she came to see me I did not feel the same childish love I felt for her growing up. I became disgusted by her presence; she made me angry because she did not have a clue what I went through as a child. All she saw was this college student who was grown. She erased my childhood out of her fucking memory. When she talked to me she acted as if everything was so fucking good, because I had the best clothes on the block growing up or because we were the only kids in the family who went to private school. She had no fucking right taking my childhood away and I did not know how to express this to her. So I tried to play her game of forgetting.

She met a new man. Smooth the Hustler was what he looked like, but his name was Chicago. He actually was from Chicago and knew how to forge checks. He was supposed to be the best in the credit card scam. He had my mother wrapped around his finger, she even called him Daddy. My mother tried real hard to connect with me; she even tried to help me decorate the house with Christmas decorations. I told her that was okay, I would rather do it alone since she was high off heroin. I know that was harsh but I wanted her to feel the rejection I felt all my life. For that one moment, she felt it. I saw it all over her face.

Heroin users bothered me. I could never tolerate the slow talking and the scratching. I wanted to continue to play the game like everything was fine but she irritated me. My skin crawled every time she talked and I noticed her arms had gotten new needle marks. At least when she was in prison she had time to let her arms heal from all the times she shot up. She never thought I had problems dealing with her drug use.

Chicago, her new man, was not interested in shooting heroin, he liked sniffing it. I thought they were the perfect couple. I did notice that he acted as if he cared for her. He did everything she asked him to do. He paid for everything and gave grandma money for Christmas. This was his first time meeting grandma and between my gifts and grandma's gifts, he spent over ten thousand dollars. All I could think of was the person or persons that they had robbed before they got to our house. I kept checking the windows while they stayed with us to see if the cops were coming.

Brandy and Christian enjoyed Christmas; I took them to see the Christmas Carol on Broadway on Christmas day. They had so many toys; they started to forget about their mother slowly. Aunt Jacky was locked up; this time she was doing state time. She was sent upstate and it was peaceful without her but I knew she would be home soon. I was relieved that she was gone. I actually was hoping that this time prison would change her since this was the first time she was serving more than 90 to 120 days.

The house was quiet, Christmas day was winding down and everyone settled into their rooms for the night. I went into my room, lit a joint and dreamed of leaving New York once I graduated college. I wanted to start a new life for myself and forget about the life I was trying to leave behind. I knew I had to first get the kids situated. Once I knew that they were all right, I would be able to leave. I knew for sure my mother could not take care of them and grandma was getting too old. I wanted them to be safe but I did not want to think that I would be stuck with them for the rest of my life. I thought I had time to think about this but time was moving fast and I had to have a plan of action if I wanted to leave without the kids. No one else was planning for the kids and this made my dream more difficult to achieve.

I played the holiday game with my mom and her new boyfriend during the week but I was ready to hang out. This was the perfect time to call Roni. My mother was there to watch the kids if I wanted to hang out, at least for the weekend. I wanted Roni to meet my officer friends. I called her and told her to meet me at the spot where all the officers hung out. I gathered all my officer friends and we met Roni in front of the spot. Roni brought her friend Melody with her. Melody was beautiful. She was my age and she had no kids. We all chipped in for a couple of grams of cocaine. We hung out at the officer's spot before going to the club that night.

We were all fly that night. I wore my new suede pants my mom got me for Christmas from Max Fifth Avenue and my new silver fox coat. We all had furs on, we looked like movie stars. At least we felt like movie stars. When we got out of Kim's car people stopped and stared at us. They wanted to know who we were; they wanted to sit at our table.

We would take turns and go into the bathroom and take a one in one cocaine hit. Big Willie's would send bottles of expensive champagne to our table and Harper would respond by giving them her number and sometimes she would leave with them. But me, I was not attracted to them. I was attracted to the material things they represented. They had cars, jewelry and the best clothes. Harper would go crazy for the guys; she would get six to seven numbers every time we went out. She loved fucking. She would leave us in a minute to fuck a cute guy with a big dick, she loved big dick. She told me once she liked to put the dick and the balls in her mouth. I know a lot of women who enjoy sucking dick but I thought balls?

Melody and I just sat and drank. We seemed to have other things on our minds after getting high. We drank and danced. Roni was having a great time, she was with Harper. They just met but they became close that night. Karen and Dee were always quiet after getting high. Karen was the only white girl and besides she was married and loved her husband. Dee hated straight clubs; he had to search harder for gay guys but he always found one by the end of the night.

I had Virgi on my mind. I tried to shake it but she was who I thought of. I did not like the idea that I was thinking about another women when I was not raised to feel like that. I never had a relationship with another woman nor did I have any gay women as friends. This feeling really came when I had too much cocaine. I would yearn for the touch of a beautiful woman. I was so ashamed of that feeling that I would try and erase it from my mind.

Addiction "Aunt Jacky"

We quickly got bored at the club and left after Dee and Harper got all the numbers they wanted. We decided to go to the nearest hotel to finish the cocaine. I was fucked up. It seemed like I was always the first one to get too high where I could not sniff anymore. My nose would freeze so fast. I would sit there and watch the girls get high and that would turn me on.

I was in a room with beautiful women and I could not fuck any of them. I used to laugh and they thought I was tripping but I was wondering which one of them I would like to luck. I definitely wasn't interested in Roni; she was too close of a friend. Kim had kids and that turned me off. Harper had too many boyfriends and she never liked for her partner to use condoms. I think she told her boyfriends to pull out when they were about to come.

Then there was Melody but I didn't know much about her. Roni introduced us that night at her house; Melody was very pretty, as they all were. But Melody was special. She seemed quiet, intellectual and confident. Melody wasn't an officer, she was an artist. She was studying for her master's degree and that did something for me. Melody had a soft-spoken voice and I was intimidated by her because I did not have a college degree. I was not used to talking with someone who had a college degree. I was in college but I was not finished. There was something different about Melody. I watched her that night and she did not respond to all the attention we were getting from the guys. I thought it was strange, I thought maybe she was in a relationship. I decided to talk with her to see what she was about.

She was so pretty. I could not help but be interested in her. She noticed me staring at her. It bothered her that I looked at her. I saw her get nervous and she asked why I kept staring at her, I could not believe what I said but I said it. I told her I could not help it, she was so good to look at. She started to unfold quickly. She blushed and my heart was beating so fast I thought it was coming out of my chest. It was a rush. I thought she would call out to me and say stop staring, but she didn't. She let me stare and I did. I noticed her perfect nose, her jet black

Indian hair, her full soft pink lips and her large breasts all in that moment.

The gang broke my concentration when they yelled out they were tired. They decided to flush the rest of the cocaine as we always did when we had enough. We did not like the idea of keeping it because when it was over we liked feeling like it was over. It was our way of dealing with the addiction; we felt if we had the strength to discard it we had the strength to stop at any time. We all were tired and we were ready to eat and go to bed. We went to the restaurant in the hotel and had breakfast and headed home.

I made sure I sat next to Melody on the way home. I laid my head on her shoulder the entire ride. She said nothing and I felt I was pushing it; but I had that urge and it would not go away. I wasn't actually ready to make love to her; I thought, I didn't know what to do if I had the opportunity. But I did need her touch that night and it was enough for me at that moment. It had to remain innocent like that so I would not feel like I was crossing over the line. That part was the hardest to face; I did not think I could handle sleeping with a woman.

The next morning I was so drained. I got up and made lunch for the kids. I kept thinking about what happened when I met Melody. I was so surprised that it happened and I enjoyed thinking about her. I was wondering when I was going to see her again. My phone rang and it was Roni. She called to say she loved the crew and she thought that the group was cool. She said she was giving a New Year's Eve party and she wanted me and the gang to come to her house. I thought it was a good idea. I asked her was Melody going to be there and she paused and asked why. I had to think quickly. I told Roni that I needed to know something about college grants. I knew Roni hated anything that had to do with college and she quickly changed the subject.

I called the gang and they all were down to hang out for New Year's at Roni's house. Karen said she would have a hard time getting out and so did Kim. Harper and Dee were down and that was all I needed since that meant I had a ride because both Dee and Harper had cars. Since I made plans for New Year's Eve, I had to make sure grandma would be off work that night. Grandma told me she would stay home, if I stayed home for her on New Year's Day. She wanted to work on New Year's Day and I wanted to hang out New Year's Eve. I was glad and excited that I was going to a New Year's Eve party. This was my first New Year's Eve Party. I had to put together an outfit and I had to get my hair done. I knew good looking guys were going to be there, as well as Melody. I had a few days before the party and I wanted to spend some of that time with the kids. I knew school was starting soon for the kids and I wanted to take them to the movies.

Christian did not start school yet, but he was anxious to get out of the house. He started to exhibit the same behavior patterns as Brandy; he would tear the house up when he was home with grandma. Christian needed to be in school, he needed to have something to do because he was becoming a hazard around the house. Spending quality time with the kids helped me a lot. I just had no knowledge on how to raise them. I only knew what I did not want them to do. I knew they needed more than what I had to offer. They needed their mother. I was into myself; I could see that I was not there for them.

It was like a brother and sister relationship. A big sister is not going to care for their little sister the way their mom would. A big sister actually wants her freedom and privacy from her siblings and that was how I always felt. But because I knew their mom was not around, I felt obligated to take them out and do things for them. It was not a motherly love type of shit; it was what I had to do. Children pick up on that shit. Both Brandy and Christian felt their separation from their mother and that's what was driving them crazy.

I had so much time off from school; I was not used to having a month off for vacation. I was able to clean my room and the house. I was used to only the two weeks off from high school.

Things were going well, grandma was not shopping as much and I felt safe. My mother was preparing to be on the road for her New Year's Eve party with Chicago. I really believed that their supply was running out and she had to re-up. She would buy dope in bundles so she would not wake up in the morning sick. She had to keep her a supply or she could not get up in the morning. Her dope addiction would have killed her if she just stopped because she shot heroin and she could never go cold turkey. That is the scariest shit; it was like she couldn't stop if she wanted to without proper help. That scared me the most about dope, I knew for sure that whatever I did in life, I would never use dope.

I was glad she met Chicago because during this visit I did not have to spend time with her. Chicago took up most of her time. He had her all over town during the day or my mother would spend time chatting with grandma at night. I purposely avoided her because she reminded me of my past and at that time I was running from it. The house was quiet again, my mother was gone, it was New Year's Eve and I was ready to party.

I cooked during the day, so when I returned grandma could go to work and I could sleep. I had the house clean and I put the kids to bed before Dee and Harper arrived. Kim called and said she would be at the party later. She wanted to spend time with her family first and Karen was doing a double shift so she was not able to hang out at all. I could not wait to get to the party and see Melody.

Everyone kept talking about how much fun we were going to have at this party. Dee and Harper had already picked up the cocaine so we were able to go straight to Roni's house. All I had to do was chip in my half. Everyone was dressed nice and ready to have a good time. Roni had redecorated the house. I have not been back to visit there since I moved backed to Brooklyn. It looked nice. I hated going to her home back in the day because it was an old house and her mother had such old furniture. Roni's new boyfriend bought all new furniture and made the house look more up-to-date. Everyone was there, even people I did not know. I was surprised Roni knew so many people. Later on I found out that those were her boyfriend's friends who were at the party. Harper and Dee found a room to go into and we started to get high and, at first, I was feeling good. The cocaine was raw and I was getting numbed quickly.

The people at the party started to make me paranoid, they were street people. Some wore long dreadlocks and walked around with spliffs hanging out of their mouths yelling, "Give praise to Allah". Then there were young men walking around with their pants hanging down and their butt cheeks sticking out. The girls wore bras as shirts and poom poom shorts. I felt out of fucking place. It appeared I was the only fucking one who felt this way because Dee and Harper left me alone. Kim did not get there yet and I could not find Melody.

I sat back and observed, as usual, and when it was time to take a one-in-one I would re-group with Dee and Harper. They were having such a good time they did not notice I wasn't. It was okay but this was the night I realized Roni and I really grew apart. She loved those people and wanted to be a part of the mix. Then it dawned on me that her boyfriend was the one yelling "give all praise to Allah!" Not only was this guy crazy, he was married and Roni knew he was married. I was surprised she allowed herself to be with someone who was married.

I kept to myself the entire party. I was feeling good from the cocaine and the wine. I brought wine with me because I knew Roni would have hard liquor and I couldn't drink the hard stuff. I began to relax and listen to the music. Melody came and sat next to me. At first, I did not know she was there and once I did, I started to feel good real fast. She must have felt something was wrong because I was sitting alone. She had bought the bill filled with cocaine with her and two glasses for the wine I brought.

We stepped into the bedroom and locked the door. She pretended the music was giving her a headache. We began to laugh at some of the people who were at the party and the clothes they were wearing. We both grabbed for the bill and Melody got it first. She took a freeze instead of a one-in-one and gave me the bill. I lit a cigarette and then took a one-in-one. I felt I had too much already so I took just a little. We both got comfortable on Roni's mother's bed.

Melody took off her shoes and started to rub her feet. She said her shoes were new and her feet hurt. I glared at her pink luscious lips while she was talking. I barely heard what she said. Her lips were so pretty I could have sucked on them; especially when she licked them. I felt I was falling in love with Melody. I felt so confused. This was all new and I was feeling good physically, but mentally it was driving me crazy. I was raised in a Baptist church; I was taught this was a sin. How could I possibly have these feelings, this must be a part of my addiction. Even though I knew this was wrong, I continued to have these feelings. I lay across the bed and Melody laid on me. She started to laugh out loud and then she told me a joke about the guy she had danced with in the other room. When she talked, I stared at her with feelings of passion and I knew she could see it. I wanted to grab her face and put my tongue down her throat. I lost my concentration when she got up to sip some wine.

I was curious about how Melody and Roni met and Melody explained that Roni works in the office next to her and they started to talk when they rode the elevator together to their office. I was trying to listen to Melody but I barely heard a word she said. I noticed while she was talking that she was missing a button on her blouse. It must have popped off when she laid across the bed because it was not like that before. A part of her blouse was open and all I could do was stare at her lace gold bra that held her perky caramel breast. My heart started to race and I couldn't move. She sipped her wine and handed me the bill, I refused. I could not sniff or take any freezes; I was numb at least for that moment. I put my wine glass down and thought to myself, I have got to kiss her. So, I moved in close to her, acting like I wanted to tell her something and I softly and slowly kissed her on the lips. I was taking a big risk but I did not care. When my lips touched hers it was mind blowing. I felt light as a feather all over, as if I was floating through the air. The kiss was wet, warm and soft and as I quickly pulled back Melody moved forward sticking her tongue in my mouth. I loved it, I could not stop. She began to move her tongue with confidence and grace, it seemed like she was experienced at this. Her lips tasted so good that I kept sucking on them. They were soft and full, nothing like a man's lips, I thought.

I opened her blouse and I got one of her breasts out of her bra and caressed her nipple. I began to suck on her breast and I knew I wanted her. I asked her to lay still; I did not want her to do anything but enjoy it. I wanted to taste her full body. I undressed her slowly and saw her beauty unfold. Her skin was soft and clear, no bumps or bruises. I licked her stomach, I touched her legs, I wanted to scream out loud but instead I cried inside with joy. She kept shaking and at one point she said "no, I can't do this". This was her first experience as it was mine but when my tongue moved slowly between her legs opening her full bodied lips she couldn't be heard.

I stroked her with my tongue and she screamed. I put my hand over her mouth and stroked her again with my tongue. Her body was trembling; this made me go deeper in her with my tongue. I felt so much control, when my tongue moved she jumped. She grabbed my head and forced me to stay down there until she was finished with me. She pushed my face so deep in her I couldn't breathe but I kept sucking and licking. She took control and I loved it. My face was soaked and I licked it off like it was chocolate cake. She pulled my hair hard and her body tightened. She came all over my face and she wrapped her legs around my head. Her body rose up off the bed and she kept jerking. I looked at her and I came.

Then there was pure silence, both of us were in shock. Melody started to dress and after she was dressed I ran to the bathroom to wash my face. No one noticed we were gone. When I came out of the bathroom Melody was in the kitchen with the other girls. The girls were eating and it was almost midnight. Roni began to fill everyone's glass with champagne and everyone gathered around for the countdown. Melody and I could not face each other; we were both embarrassed by what we did. It was ten seconds before the ball was going to drop and Roni decided to couple people up so they would have someone to kiss. I just had pussy in my mouth, I was not eager to kiss anyone. The ball dropped and I toasted my glass and was ready to go home. I was tired and I felt uncomfortable being there.

Harper, Dee and Kim were not ready to go. Since Kim got there late she was ready to party. I decided to call a cab and Melody asked if she could ride with me since she knew she was going to be drinking and decided not to bring her car. I was glad Melody asked to ride with me. It was late and I asked Melody to stay at my house since we needed to talk and she agreed. When we got to my house we tiptoed to my bedroom, undressed and got into bed. We talked; we had to get it off our chest. We knew we were not ready to commit to the feelings we had for one another. None of our friends were gay. Dee was gay but he was scared to come out. So we did not consider him as being gay. Our families would have been against it and neither of us could handle the pressure. So that night we kissed, hugged and felt the beauty of each other's body. I was wrapped in Melody's beautiful skin and I felt so relaxed. I never felt so much comfort and tranquility in my life. That was the one thing I loved about Melody, she allowed me to express how I felt about her. She allowed me to express who I really was and she loved that I fell in love with her. Melody loved hearing it and that was one of the best nights of my life.

Chapter 11

Feelings Change

Grandma's birthday was getting closer and she was still working. I thought I would have lost her by now. She was turning 69 years old and her job was forcing her to retire and she tried to fight it. Grandma could not drive any longer because she had gotten too old to drive. She had to take public transportation to work. But the funny thing about it was, she did not care; she would wait outside for the bus with her walking stick. I think it bothered me more than it bothered her. It would kill me that she had to do that. I remember begging her to stay home and she wouldn't. I used to watch her while she waited for the bus in the cold. She was determined and no matter what anyone said she kept on until her employer told her it was time for her to quit.

She was devastated. She came home and cried. She said, "This is it, this is what life offers you". I will never forget those words, she was distraught. All she did was work and when she got too old no one wanted her. She had nothing to show that she worked all her life. She had no property, no car, and no real money in the bank. Her children were not around to help her. Grandma could not retire and live comfortably in her own home because she was renting and since my brother died she felt useless.

Grandma felt this way because she had loads of energy. She loved getting up in the morning and having somewhere to go. I couldn't stand to watch her like this so I decided to call my mother and I told her to contact Aunt Jacky. Since Aunt Jacky was just released after doing her bid I wanted her to come and talk with grandma. My mother was glad to hear from me. She knew I never called unless I needed something. The next day my mother came over along with Aunt Jacky and they took grandma to Atlantic City. They spent thousands of dollars in Atlantic City gambling and showing grandma a good time.

My mother had a fresh set of stolen checks she was dying to use. She cashed them in Atlantic City and my Grandma loved it. Grandma fell in love with the casinos. She played the quarter slot machines and she won twenty five hundred dollars. When Grandma came home she was so happy; she seemed like a different person. She needed to go to Atlantic City to see other senior citizens. She met some people who lived in the senior citizens building where she used to work. These people went to Atlantic City twice a month and grandma agreed to go back with them. I was happy she found some friends. She even started to call them and they would talk for hours. I never knew grandma to talk on the phone, let alone go out for fun.

Aunt Jacky was there after the trip and I tried to meet with her regarding the kids. I knew she was just released from prison a couple of weeks ago and I needed her to start interacting with her kids. She was supposed to be in a drug program to kick her addictions. This was one of the conditions of her release. Aunt Jacky quickly became inpatient when I tried to talk to her about the kids. She pushed me away and said she will talk about this later. I told her I was going to graduate college sooner than I thought and she needs to make plans for the kids. Aunt Jacky told me "to get the fuck out of her face". I knew she did not love her kids and whatever I did was not enough. She was a selfish inconsiderate BITCH who only cared for herself.

When she was around Brandy and Christian did not even notice her. They were so attached to me and grandma and that was the problem. I knew Aunt Jacky was just doing this program shit because she had to; she had no real interest in attending the program. She was still getting high while she was in the program. She knew how to clean her system before her counselor tested her for drugs. I was angry that she was not interested in her kids, which led to who will care for her kids?

I quickly became depressed thinking about my future with the kids, I had no idea what was I going to do. I knew I could not talk with grandma about this problem; she had already planned on caring for the kids until the day she died. That was not an issue for her. I was doing well in school but my home life was eating me up. I was becoming more frustrated with my situation. The drugs did not help as it did in the past but I continued to use them anyway. I was not getting that good feeling anymore. It became an ADDICTION. The gang and I were using more and more cocaine.

Melody and I were growing apart. She met a psychologist who worked in her office. She really seemed to like him and I could not stand in her way and act jealous. I pretended to be happy for her and moved on. Melody and I knew we were not ready to be involved and that night basically was something we both wanted to experience. It was not a secret that we were scared to live life as lesbians. That made me realize who I was and what I wanted in life. I realized that I needed to be straight in order to live as everyone else. I felt I had enough problems and that would have caused more. But I knew deep down inside that whatever my mouth said had nothing to do with what my body was responding to.

I regrouped and got myself together because I knew even if I was stuck with the kids I had to have an education. I concentrated on my school work and focused harder.

The gang was going uptown to get cocaine more often and I was getting tired of it. I invested so many years in getting high it became difficult to let go. Getting high was my security blanket and I continued to convince myself that I could stop when I was ready. Deep down inside I was ready to stop but I could not stop. I was scared to tell the gang I was ready to quit going uptown and buying cocaine. I continued to go ahead with them even though I wasn't enjoying the high anymore. I had no idea that this decision would cost me my friendships.

We continued with our same routine, first we would buy a couple of grams and sniff cocaine until our nose froze. It started to become impossible to throw the rest away like before. It got to the point where we had to sniff every drop and sometimes we went back to buy more. By the time the first round was finished I was too high to go back uptown. But we would drive all the way back to get a few more grams of cocaine. We were sniffing cocaine until morning. We would end up in little dark places where correctional and state officers would hang out. I saw myself falling to a place that I knew was wrong for me. I used to associate cocaine with ballers and go-getters, but I then started to see them as low-life losers. I did not want to be like that and it was tearing me apart.

One thing I realized about growing up in addiction; stopping is never an option. Even if you get a good job or go to college, you are trapped. I know people who I have grown up with, who have done positive things in their lives but they cannot leave behind the addiction to drugs, alcohol and sex. Drugs and alcohol become a part of who they really are. That is why only a few beat their ADDICTIONS. I felt even though I was in college the addiction was in me and on me. I felt no change in my life. I had no strength, no courage, and no confidence. I was weak. The clothes, cocaine and the popular friends gave me courage but did nothing for my emotional state. I knew what I was doing was wrong and I had to get my shit together. It seemed like the higher I got, the more I focused on school. It was the guilt of getting high; I guess I had to feel like I was doing something right.

School was ending and I was glad. I was exhausted. I needed to sleep and that was the one thing I could not get. I had to go to summer school if I planned on getting out of school early. I wanted to graduate a year earlier than I planned since my study group was already one year ahead of me. I wanted to graduate with them instead of doing four years. I decided to double up and get out in three years. I was tired, but I was also excited that I had a chance to get out of college early. That motivated me even more; I had big dreams for when I graduated college. I wanted to move away, buy a car and start a new life. I wanted to stop the addiction, the addiction to drugs and the addiction to my family. I was studying psychology. I loved it. It helped me deal with my family problems and I was getting A's for the first time in my life.

The gang had a lot of work to catch up on so our hanging out was getting in the way. They decided to hang only on the weekends instead of during the weekdays like we had been doing. They had to do doubles, cover other workers shifts, and they also needed their rest. This was great for me, I wanted to slow down. I was getting so tired of getting high off of cocaine every day. This gave me time to spend with grandma and the kids.

Christian was in school, so it was easier than before. I was glad both kids were in school. The house stayed clean longer and I was able to have peace of mind during the day when I did not have class. When school was finished for the kids, I made plans to register them into summer camp full-time. Brandy and Christian were growing so fast, they were practically taking care of themselves. We rented movies and played games. My life was full between school, the kids and hanging out.

I did not have time to date. I remembered that I met a guy at the club, he was very handsome. I had his number for weeks before I decided to call because I hadn't dated a guy since Sean the nerd and I had not had sex since Melody. His name was Jon. I tried to remember how he looked and all I could remember was him looking like a dog. I did not care though; I was not looking for a relationship. I just wanted to have some fun. I missed feeling attracted to someone and since I decided that I was not going to be with a woman I needed to feel what it was like to date a man again.

I called Jon and we spoke briefly on the phone and he offered to take me out to dinner. He was nice over the phone and he sounded like a strong black man. He was a computer programmer and he recently graduated from college and I was impressed. He had no kids but he did live at home with his mother. I did not mind, I lived at home as well.

He picked me up at the train station because I did not want to tell him where I lived. I was smiling when he picked me up because he had a nice car and he looked good. During the car ride we were both quiet, it was like we knew each other's intentions. I certainly did not expect anything spectacular to happen since I had been sitting on his number for weeks and never called. He probably thought I wanted a free meal and I thought he just wanted some pussy. So, he took me to a fancy restaurant to eat and he was very kind and gentle. After a few glasses of wine, he started to become more communicative. I enjoyed talking with him. I like him right off the back. After dinner we went to a bar & grill and had some drinks. He was very generous and he bought me whatever I wanted that evening.

I was impressed, especially by the way he smelled. I was falling for him. He asked me to dance when Marvin Gaye's song came on and we slow danced to "Let's get it on". I felt him rising and it turned me on. I haven't felt this way about a man in a long time. He looked so good. I kissed him slowly and as I was kissing him I felt him get hard as a rock. I was turned on immediately. He whispered in my ear and asked me if I wanted to go to a hotel. I said, "Yes". We got our coats and drove to the nearest hotel. He got the nicest room with the Jacuzzi. Jon ordered some drinks and lit a joint.

We vibed for a minute before his true colors came out. He talked about himself mostly and I gave little information about myself because I did not want him to know much about me, since I knew this would be a one night stand. He smoked a lot and I noticed myself trying to keep up with him. I was glad he smoked weed and not cocaine and I was enjoying smoking the weed with him. It helped me to relax.

I wasn't paying him any attention because I was zoning out off the weed. As I was relaxing, I noticed he started to talk a little more aggressively and this caught my attention. Then he became violent, I mean rough. At first it turned me on. I normally got weak when a man shoved his tongue down my throat. So I let him push me around for a minute before I realized his eyes had lit up like fire balls when he grabbed me by the throat and choked the shit out of me. I was surprised and I sobered up quickly. He punched me in the head and I must have passed out. I awoke finding him undressing me and I tried to fight him but he was too strong.

He took off all his clothes and stood over me laughing. I thought to myself this motherfucker is crazy. He said, "I didn't mean to hurt you but I wanted to let you know who was in control". He actually tried to be gentle after that. I wanted to run out of the room without any clothes on but he pinned me to the bed. He started to put a condom on and I became filled with relief because he wasn't trying to fuck raw.

I looked at his DICK as he was trying to put the condom on and saw something that scared the shit out of me. His DICK was so fucking big. I thought to myself, this is something I was not used to. I thought if he put that in my mouth it will come through my throat. I begged him not to put it in, that shit was not human. I thought he had to be deformed. He knew his DICK was too big for me so he tried to fuck me while standing over me. It physically hung to his knees. I could not believe what I saw; my pussy is and has always been tight. I never experienced something like that and I was not prepared to experience it this time. He tried to put it in but I closed my legs tight as I could and he barely got the tip in. He tried his best to force it and I guessed it turned him on because he came, the condom filled up like a water balloon.

I could not wait to get dressed and get the hell out of there. I didn't want him to take me home. We were both quiet as I dressed. He lay in bed with a dumb ass look on his face. I ran out the room and jumped into a cab without saying anything. He had the nerve to call me once I got home to see if I wanted to go out with him again. I hung up on him and was ready to change my phone number if he tried calling again. That night I didn't cry, I was surprised. I lay in bed, smoked a joint and meditated. I was feeling lucky even though I was humiliated and stripped of my pride. I was alive and at that moment I now hated men more than before. I never had any luck with men. I was twenty years old and I, at that moment, knew I would never be able to have a functional relationship with a man until I knew what I wanted as a young woman.

I actually felt stronger at this point in my life. I realized that men cannot fulfill the love I was looking for. I needed to start loving myself if I wanted to feel good about myself. Jon was only being who he was and I was doing what I thought women do on a one night stand. I was not happy with that type of life style but there was something about it that kept drawing me to these types of people. I knew the addiction was part of it and that is why I knew I had to stop if I ever wanted to really make a change in my life. I had to stop getting high. I did not know how to stop, even if I wanted to; but I thought more and more about it and it started to become real for me. I looked at my life and all the mistakes I made were because of my addiction. I was so dependent on weed I did not consider stopping that first. I wanted to first get off the cocaine then I planned to get off the weed.

I knew I would have to tell the gang I was going to stop sniffing cocaine before they called and made plans with me. I just couldn't bring myself to tell them. So, I did the next best thing, I avoided them when they called. I did not answer their calls and if I did answer I acted as if I was sick. I could not play that game too long before they got suspicious. These were officers and I did not want to make them think I was pulling out. If I pulled out they would think I would turn on them and report them. My life could be in danger just because I wanted to stop using cocaine.

Chapter 12

The End of the Beginning

I was able to stay away for six weeks; I have not sniffed any cocaine in six weeks. I was having shakes at night; my body was hurting all over. My bones ached for days and all I did for six weeks was smoke weed every day to help rid my addiction to cocaine. I sniffed cocaine for over two years straight and I decided to stop cold turkey. It was one of the most painful experiences I ever had to go through. The crying at night for no reason freaked me out, the suicidal ideas scared me. I actually thought about killing myself. Then I started to lose weight and everyone thought I was sick.

I thought I was rid of my street friends but they had something else planned for me. Since I did not return their calls, they decided to bring the party to my home one night. I was shocked. It was 11 p.m. on a Saturday night. I went to bed early, something I started getting used to doing. My doorbell rang. I was scared to open the door because we never have visitors past 10 p.m., especially, if I am not hanging out. I told grandma to stay in bed and I would get the door. I ran downstairs and opened the door and to my surprise, there was Melody, Kim, Dee, Harper and Roni. I was not in the mood; but they were so pushy that they let themselves in quietly and went straight to our hangout spot in my house, which was the basement. I tried telling the gang that I was not in the mood but they took the dollar bill out crushed some cocaine and started pouring cocaine on it. My eyes lit up and my mouth went dry. I was fighting the urge for the cocaine. I was clean for six weeks and those six weeks at that moment seemed like one day. I grabbed the bill and stared at it and I started to remember the night I was sick all alone fighting my addiction to cocaine. In my mind I kept saying six weeks, six weeks.

The gang wanted to go out and I did not want to go. I did not see me with the gang anymore but they failed to see it. They failed to see my need to stop getting high. We then moved to my room and they started to take my clothes out of my closet and told me to get dressed because they are not leaving without me. I realized they were serious and I could get hurt if I did not go with them. I tried telling them I was babysitting but they knew I was lying. Especially, since my grandmother had yelled out wanting to know who was at the door when they arrived? They must have heard her.

I do not know why I did not have the strength to stop them right there. I truly did not want to go. For the first time in my life, I felt torn. I had six weeks of being clean under my belt and I was ready to go all the way. I decided to get dressed because I saw they were not giving up and I wanted them out of my house. While dressing, I kept telling myself that I was not going to get high with them. I was just going for the ride. They quickly announced that they were not going to the club; they were going to the spot where all the officers were hanging out so I did not have to get dressed up. I threw on my jeans and a t-shirt and went for the ride.

During the car ride I was very quiet. Melody was the only one in the crew that noticed. I could not even look at her. She tried to make conversation but I was not interested. All I wanted to do was get this night over with. We finally got to the spot and it was darker than usual. I never noticed that before but it was pitch black. Everyone found seats where there were lit candles and started to pass the bill. I lit a cigarette and pretended I went already. I did this practically all night. I looked at everyone, observing them with the keenest eye. Looking at how the drugs affected them in some way or another. They did not think they showed signs of being high but I saw the ADDICTION full blown on everyone's face. The hunger to escape, the need to feel something else was visible to me that night. I knew that feeling all too well. I kept thinking to myself, what have I done with my life? Everyone looked happy, but I kept thinking to myself that I could not have been the only one in there wanting to get out of this life.

I looked up and I saw a familiar face walk through the door. Even though it was dark, this face I recognized. It was a woman and she started to walk towards me smiling like she knew me. As she got closer, I became more nervous and I realized that she was no stranger, it was Aunt Jacky. She came to the spot to get high. I froze when she said, "What's up!" I could not say a word. I was there and she saw me. When I looked at her all I could feel was disgust. Not for her but disgust with myself. I was running from her all my life and because of the life I chose, I ended up right back with Aunt Jacky in a place I thought I could escape Aunt Jacky. She sat down and ironically she knew my friends. They passed the bill to her and I looked at her with amazement. I knew my life would be fucked up if I took that bill because I will become Aunt Jacky. I will never change, I will lose.

I stood up at the table and told the gang I was leaving. They did not hear me as I headed towards the door. I turned around for a last look because I was never going to be there again in my life. As I headed towards the door, Melody called me and sincerely asked where I was going; and I told her this was not for me. I couldn't do this any longer. I saw something that night I never saw and that was ADDICTION. She looked at me with a sad face as if she wanted to go with me, but I knew she couldn't leave the high. I was not mad at her, I understood that feeling and I said nothing to her. I could not judge her.

I finally got out of the door and a calm feeling of relief came over me. I went to the street to hail a cab and as I stood in the street staring at the spot, I cried. I cried about all the years I wasted in the spot, all the years I wasted getting high. Melody came to the door and watched as I waved my hand for a taxi. I looked at her while waving for a taxi, at the same time hoping she would run to me. We locked eyes and I noticed her eyes were sad. I wanted to go back for her, but I couldn't. As soon as the taxi stopped, I felt I had no choice but to get in the taxi. I got into the taxi still looking at Melody. At the same time, I noticed white men running towards the spot with guns. I started to look around and I noticed that cops cars were pulling up two and three at a time. They were all running into the spot where the crew was and I could not warn them. When the cops ran in with their guns drawn the officers inside must have panicked and thought it was a stick up because I began to hear different sounds of gun fire as I saw people running out of the club and being shot. I screamed so loud that the cab driver sped off and all I could see was smoke from the bullets being fired in the air.

To be continued...

About the Author

Rana Ryan was born in Brooklyn, New York; she was raised in Queens, New York where she studied Psychology and earned her Bachelor's degree. Right out of college Rana Ryan worked with children and families who suffered profoundly from addiction, abuse, abandonment and imprisonment. This is where she witnessed how the crack error destroyed families, financially, emotionally and spiritually.

Rana Ryan then went back to school earning her first master's degree, Masters in Public Administration. From there she managed foster care and preventive programs seeing how families with addiction were treated and how they became addicted to drugs. Here, Rana Ryan witnessed the ramifications of drug use in families, children separated from their families, parents imprisoned and abuse on the rise.

Rana Ryan decided again to go back to school to earn yet another degree , a Master in Business Administration, where she learned how to manage and operate her own business affording her the opportunity to consult for many of the top family agencies in New York City.

This opportunity afforded Rana Ryan a chance to train social workers on how to work with families who have been broken due to long term drug use.

After much request from her past and current clients, Rana Ryan went back to earn her third and last degree, Master in Social Work leading her to take the state board exam allowing her to practice as a licensed therapist. This is where Rana Ryan best work was achieved, working with families and children who suffered because of addiction. Addiction Aunt Jacky was born out of all the work Rana Ryan had the opportunity to do with the families she served.

Addiction Aunt Jacky is an urban novel that focuses on the powerful introduction to drug use in America from the beginning. Rana Ryan wanted to capture the behaviors, the shame, the cycle and the obstacles that come with addiction; Rana Ryan exposed in this book how addiction can be good and bad, depending on your drug of choice. Addiction Aunt Jacky powerfully address what a child goes through once exposed to drug use without limitations. Rana Ryan wanted her readers to see the narrow choices children have when exposed to drugs and how making decisions to get off drugs is one of the hardest decisions to make.

Rana Ryan, LMSW, MBA, MPA-CAMF

Phone: 646-462-1026

Email: Addictionauntjacky@gmail.com

Website: www.ConsultwithRanaRyan.com

Podcast: https://anchor.fm/addiction-aunt-jacky

https://play.radiopublic.com

https://www.stitcher.com

https://www.breaker.audio

https://pca.st/SjeQ.

Addiction "Aunt Jacky"

ORDER FORM

Please email orders to:

Addictionauntjacky@gmail.com

Please send _____ Copies of Addiction Aunt Jacky

Name: _____

Address: _____

City: _____ State: _____ Zip: _____

Tele phone: (____)_____/ (____)_____

Email: _____

I have enclosed $14.99, plus $7.00 shipping per book for a total of $_____.

Sales Tax: Add 8.875% to total cost of books for orders shipped to NY addresses.

For further information about this book or for appearances, you can reach Rana Ryan at: 646-462-1026 or email her at: Addictionauntjacky@gmail.com

Visit: www.ConsultwithRanaRyan.com for further information

Addiction "Aunt Jacky"

www.ingramcontent.com/pod-product-compliance
Lightning Source LLC
Chambersburg PA
CBHW072337300426
44109CB00042B/1661